This book is dedicated to everyone who
has patiently listened to me talk about chocolate,
word by word, chapter by chapter. A very
special thanks to my favorite
chocolate Marcia Prentice for her
undying support and love.
Of course to my loving mother Effie Miner.
And my wonderful sons Loren and Alex
I love you.

Foreword ~

From world famous stars and politicians to everyday people with extraordinary stories, it is my job as a television journalist to unlock celebrity secrets and earn the trust of those from all walks of life. I am surprised to hear some of the intimate issues most are willing to disclose, especially when it comes to their lives and love. And who doesn't reveal personal details to their hairdresser that they would never think to tell a friend or colleague?

I, like Anthony Miner, have found myself serving as a sounding board for those trying to interpret, understand and fashion deep, meaningful relationships. I know firsthand, sitting in a salon chair is at times just as rewarding as lying on a therapist's couch. As an incredibly talented stylist for countless celebrities, Anthony has served as a counselor and confidant to many women and men alike. I have seen his unique ability to objectively offer invaluable in sight and sound advice when it comes to matters of the heart. This book sets some basic guidelines for those who wonder how to control their cravings for relationships and when it is ok to indulge.

One late night, buried beneath some old receipts and cards, I discovered a chocolate heart. It was shining in gold foil, carefully placed on a creamy velvet cushion and securely enclosed in an antique, glass box. It was just as the day I received it, years ago. When Anthony asked me to write the forward for this book, it brought me back to that time. That little sparking piece of candy was a gift from my Jake, whom you will meet in the following pages. Ironically, he often told

If You Like Chocolate
Eat Chocolate

If You Like Chocolate Eat Chocolate

Learn How To Manage The Chocolate You Desire

~

Anthony Miner

Drop Street Press.LLC

www.ifyoulikechocolateeatchocolate.com

If You Like Chocolate Eat Chocolate is a registered trademark of Drop Street Press LLC.

Designed by Lorenzo

Published by BookSurge

Library of Congress Cataloging-in-Publication
Miner, Anthony.
If You Like Chocolate Eat Chocolate: learn to manage the chocolate you desire / Anthony Miner

ISBN 1-4196-8880-4
   1.Miner, Anthony – Relationship   2. Self help – Relationship – 3. Women – Relationship. I. Title

Printed in the United States of America.

First Edition: April 2008
10 9 8 7 6 5 4 3 2 1

me, "you are just like chocolate." Admittedly, it is a lovely thought, but I never fully understood the extent of its meaning. It was Anthony who helped me realize that such a simple metaphor holds a world of significance.

What is chocolate-an addiction... a decadent secret... a sinful indulgence? Presenting itself in all different shapes, sizes and textures, it can be bitter and even at times, bland. Some chocolate lasts a lifetime if you know how to keep it, but most will melt away if held too tightly. The pages of this book provide a simple approach toward achieving the relationship you desire and help you to write your own recipe for sweet success.

Victoria Recaño Host –
The Insider and *Entertainment Tonight*

Acknowledgements ~

The day I started writing this book, I knew I had a story to tell. I needed to share a point of view that I felt was missing in the arena of women's self-help relationship books. As cliché as it may sound, my years working as a hair stylist have helped me to understand women's behavioral needs. Although, since I was a kid, I have always had insight and interest in human relationships. As an adult, I am fortunate to be a great communicator and women trust me.

One morning while at work around 7:00AM, the leading actress on a television show sat in my chair for me to style her hair for her first scene. About ten minutes into her hair she began to cry. I thought to myself, "Is she crying about the hairstyle? I'm just getting started. Or…Is she crying over the television script?" Well, it didn't take long to discover that she was crying over her boyfriend - her chocolate. She isn't the first client to shed tears over a man, in front of me and certainly not the last. I had a client who would show up out of the blue – no appointment – just show up for a haircut. After her "hellos" her next words were "cut it off." I learned to interpret "cut it off" to mean cut him off; her hair as a symbolism of her now ex. After listening to all of my female client's stories, I learned something new about women's needs and desires. As I saw the pattern of what women really needed and wanted, I also saw an opportunity to help them sort out these things we call love and relationships. I made the transition from stylist to relationship coach.

My original goal was to be the best hairstylist for them. Looking back, as they confided in me and I gave them advice, my hair therapy sessions outgrew my hairstyling business. For my clients, I am their voice of reason and non-judgment. My stance is never to judge what a person does or doesn't do. If you have an unusual fetish, more power to you. If you like your chocolate served the way you like it, I'm not one to judge because we all like what we like. This attitude might be one of the keys to my success with my relationship coaching and hopefully will lead to this book being a huge success.

Having success with my inner circle of clients, I decided to take my experience, wisdom, and knowledge and share it with the world. After about eighteen months of non-stop writing and rewriting and rewriting, *If You Like Chocolate Eat Chocolate* is finished.

With that, I would like to thank every woman that let me help resolve some conflicts in her relationship. I want to thank my inner circle of friends, and clients whom I consulted on a weekly basis regarding their current relationships. Also, the women that was curious enough about *If You Like Chocolate Eat Chocolate* to listen to some of my ideas. I want to send a thank you to Marcia Prentice, who patiently listened to me explain every point in this book over and over again. Your patience is applauded; thank you for being the first to add "*If You Like Chocolate Eat Chocolate*" as a favorite book. And a special thank you to my mother, who is my favorite critic. It's not that she is critical, but she is a very honest person. If she likes it, she likes it, no b.s. Needless to say, she loves this book. Thanks Mom, I love you.

Finally, to all the women who have crossed my life path for good or bad, thank you. Without those experiences, I would never have written this book or become the man I am today.

The Table of Contents

Foreword

Acknowledgement

Chocolate ~

"All I really need is love, but a little chocolate now and then doesn't hurt!" - Lucy Van Pelt (in Peanuts, by Charles M. Schulz)

Introduction

Over the years, I have spent hours listening to my female friends and family rant, and rarely rave about the men in their relationships. It is always the same issues regardless of age, class, race, ethnic background, or religion. Their complaints are as follows: "Why didn't he call back after sex?" "Now that we've had sex what does that mean?" "He cheated on me! I thought we were exclusive?" "He doesn't listen." "He's being a jerk." "He's a dog." "He can't be trusted." "I should move on." "I can do better." "He's a loser." And so on.

I thought to myself, wow, what is going on here? Most of my life I wondered whether men are really that bad? Am I that guy? Who are these men women are talking about? All of my male friends and family members seem like decent guys. Are they talking about them? Or is it me they are talking about? Then I thought, what is the common denominator among all women in relationships that is causing so much resentment towards men? Is it that women are more sensitive than men? Are men just impervious to women's needs? Are men and women just incompatible? As an adult, I then realized that women's frustration with men stems from never being taught how to manage their relationships. Women are not taught how to manage or behave in a relationship with a man to get their desired results. When a woman's needs are not being met and her partner is behaving contrary to her expectations, of course the end result is – "He's a jerk, I can do better."

Although, there are women in great relationships and are having their needs met, I'm not sure this can be said about the majority of women that are in the dating scene. This is not to say men don't have their share of responsibility for a relationship, they do. But keep in mind, this book is written for women to understand men's behavior.

Just as a woman battles with her weight due to compulsive or simply incorrect eating habits, the same lack of knowledge and discipline affect her behavior in a relationship. As a child she is never taught how to eat in moderation, what foods are better for her than others, what healthy serving sizes are for all three meals, and what are the side effects of soda, sugar, coffee, and fast food. She is also not taught how to enjoy her chocolate in moderation without getting cavities. It is no wonder that Americans are overweight and women are frustrated in love.

When a young woman enters a relationship, she is not taught how to love or not love a man. Nor is she taught the habits of men. What are the dos and don'ts of relationships? What are men's emotional and physical needs? Unfortunately, she is not given the best examples from her parents either, specifically from her father. She leaves home at eighteen with a pat on the back and the words *"good luck"* as she goes into the world of relationships unprepared. When she arrives in the world of dating, it's a free for all – on the job training if you will, on how to be in a relationship with a man. She'll bounce from relationship to relationship learning lessons from the ebb and flow of love, and losing faith in her dreams of romance and love. By the time she is twenty-five, she is frustrated and confused about men and what they want. Along her path she does her best to please him in exchange for some type of validation and connection. The virile male has a different motivation. His agenda is to conquer his quests, sow his oats, and take no prisoners. Sensitivity training is not in his vocation, leaving the innocent and naïve eighteen-year-old girl gasping for ways to shield her heart and feelings.

This common trait of bad relationship management is not exclusive to my inner circle of family and friends. This thread is woven worldwide and is the number one conflict women have in their relationships. The conflict arises the moment a woman's relationship doesn't develop the way she expected, which is based on her minimal information about men. She is taught that if a man loves her he should never look at another woman with lust in his eyes. She wants him to read her mind, because if he really cared he would know what she is feeling! She gives him sex and thinks that by doing so he agrees that they are in a relationship. These are a few examples of impossible feats that some women hold close to their heart as truths.

According to my theory, there are two types of men - Chocolate and Salad. Most women are attracted to Chocolate and are bored with Salad. Besides not understanding male behavior, the root of most conflicts in a relationship stem from the fact that women want their chocolate to behave like salad.

My definition of Chocolate and Salad:

Chocolate – *The Bad Boys, the unattainable guys of the world. The guys with an edge, who take risks, willing to break the rules, drive fast cars, are charming, and sexy. These men are not necessarily emotionally, available nor are they looking for a commitment. At the very least this is persona. Hollywood's Chocolate includes. Jack Nickelson, Colin Farrell, Johnny Depp, George Clooney, Gene Simmons, Vin Diesel, Tommy Lee Jones, and Tupac, to name a few. Considering most of us don't hang out in this Hollywood circle, let's identify the chocolate in your circle. He is the wannabe rock star musician, the smooth talking pretty boy with the six pack and tattoos, the arrogant cocky guy at your gym, or the womanizer in your night club scene who could care less about you or your feelings. Or he's your present boyfriend, the one where you are always footing the bill for dinner and other entertainment. Another way to define chocolate is that he is the one guy you're emotionally addicted to.*

As chocolate lovers, we all have our favorite pieces of rich, luscious, sumptuous sculptures. Some of us like pure milk chocolate, dark rich chocolate, white chocolate, mint, fudge, creamy, and/or sugar free chocolate. Whichever the form, we are all vulnerable to its addiction.

Salad – *Mr. Nice Guys of the world that resemble Ron Howard, Tom Hanks, Ryan Seacrest, Nick Lachey, and Justin Timberlake. Much like a dish of raw leafy green vegetables often tossed with pieces of other raw or cooked vegetables, they are good for you. Not very exciting and nor do they release your endorphins. These are truly the good guys of the* *world: trustworthy, honest, honorable, and loyal. This is not to say that chocolate can't be trusted. What I am saying is that salad can never replace chocolate.* There is nothing wrong with being a gentleman; however, it's just that most women find Mr. Nice guy boring.

Unlike chocolate, salad is predictable and healthy. Salad will take mental notes or write down important dates. Salad wants to please you and make you happy as much as possible and is emotionally available when you call. He wants your validation. On the other hand, you want to please your chocolate by any means necessary. Chocolate is more self-indulgent and more likely to forget important dates. In general, chocolate ultimately makes you low on his list of priorities. Chocolate does not acknowledge your important days and only wants to see you at 2AM, after he has been clubbing and has left you tapping your fingers until he arrives. You think to yourself. "Why can't he remember the date we met and surprise me with a candlelit dinner at least once a year? I do not want to be the late night 2AM booty call. I want my chocolate to behave like salad and it never happens."

This reminds me of a story I once heard about a man who complained to the pet store manager about a cat he had recently purchased. The man went back to the pet shop and told the manager that the cat is scratching the couch with his paws and climbing up and down the drape's and isn't coming when he called his name. He is very independent. The pet store manager is baffled. He said okay, but what is your complaint with the cat. The man sighed, and then said, "My dog didn't act like that."

Sometimes we have an expectation that someone's demeanor should change to accommodate our needs and desires. We want chocolate to behave like salad and salad to behave like chocolate, at our convenience. Chocolate and salad each have their own rules, behavior, and agenda just as cats and dogs. Salad is Chocolate's nemesis. Neither you nor I can change that, but you can appreciate their differences and enjoy them for what they are worth.

There are many books and television programs on the subject of relationships between the sexes. Some books insist you stop eating chocolate all together. They shriek, "Eat a fresh salad its good for you." Others tell women to follow the rules to get your chocolate to behave like salad. Another says that your chocolate is just not into you. Whether these books, magazines, or television shows are helpful or not, the bottom line is you like what you like. The media doesn't explain the how's and why's of our attraction to chocolate. They insist there is something wrong with your chocolate and you for liking it. They even convince you to change your expectations of chocolate that it can behave in other ways other than chocolate. That never works. Chocolate doesn't live up to the expectations you are told to expect by your girlfriends, psychologists, talk show hosts, and relationship experts. When that doesn't work you thoughts go as such, "I can do better, he's not the one," "It's not my fault, he doesn't appreciate a good women." "Don't settle I'll find my Mr. Right." By the way who is this Mr. Right!

These media ideologies never made sense to me. Why should we toss away the things we like and want? You wouldn't toss out a great pair of shoes you love because someone said you could do better. Why should we change the things we like, especially the people we are most attracted to? Is it really possible to stop liking men that are dark-skinned and tall with an Italian accent and a great muscular body and make yourself attracted to the loveable, short, bald, and overweight guy? Is it possible to stop liking designer jeans and settle for Lee's straight leg jeans? I don't think so. Although you might change for the understudy, your heart will always desire your chocolate that got away.

I believe if you learn how to manage your chocolate, the thought of changing your chocolate will never cross your mind. Let's be honest, who wants to throw away a perfectly good mouth watering Godiva Hazelnut Praline Truffle just because? The answer is no one wants to. Hence, the book - *If You Like* **Chocolate** *Eat* **Chocolate***;* Learning to manage the chocolate that you desire.

This book is written to give women the bottom line between the sexes; the how, the what, and the why? I want to explain why women are attracted to chocolate. What is it about chocolate that mesmerizes women? Where did these triggers of attraction for chocolate come from? Why do women like chocolate vs. green salads? How do you manage chocolate without gaining weight, getting pimples, or getting sick? In addition, women will learn where salad fits into their lives.

A lot of women get wrong information about how men think and feel from the wrong sources - other women. Of course, not all women give wrong advice. Women become cheerleaders for each other versus a voice of reason. For one, she isn't a man and more importantly, her emotions can get in the way. Women tend to put themselves in the emotional state of the advice they are giving. If one woman is giving her friend advice on what to do about a guy that hasn't called her in three days, the friend that is giving the advice will recall her experience in a similar situation. While in that emotional state, she gives her friend emotional advice instead of logical advice, which more than likely logical advice is what the situation needs. The advice she gives her friend to resolve the issue is usually unfavorable toward the man. She pinpoints the man's behavior as that of a jerk and never makes her friend somewhat accountable for the outcome or helps her to see her actions objectively.

Another factor affecting the advice you receive from a girlfriend is that she could very well be jealous because you have a man. While on the other hand, she is home replying to emails from *match.com* and watching *Sex in the City* reruns. Whatever the reasons, sometimes a logical voice is what a woman needs to hear to put the issue into perspective, not a girlfriend who wants to vent about her own frustrations with men.

Mistakenly, women ask enigmatic questions... "What does it mean?" He didn't call – "What does it mean?" "He said I was special and the only one – What does it mean?" In the end her girlfriend's advice doesn't resolve the issue, but only exacerbates more conflict and ill feeling toward men. When she hears her advisors say - "Leave him, move on." " He's a dog; men are jerks." "Once a cheater always a cheater." Needing some comfort and company, she agrees, but in her heart there is no way she is going to let her chocolate go that easily. All the male bashing in the world is not going to let her walk away. The addiction is too strong and besides if he calls, she is going to find a way to forgive him. Better yet, she will find the right excuse to forgive him.

So what does it mean? Simply put nothing more than the words themselves. If he says, "I love you," it means "I love you." If he didn't call for three days, that simply means you are not a priority. No more, no less. It doesn't mean he doesn't wants to get married or you are not attractive. Women want to believe there is more meaning behind his words or some hidden message. There isn't… To make it even simpler, his actions do speak much louder than his words.

I did my best to simplify the contents of this book. As I wrote these pages I kept in mind that I wanted a fourteen to fifty-year-old to understand these simple concepts. Obviously, a fourteen-year-old is too young to have the experiences in some of these topics. The point is that I wanted to take out the complications of relationships which we are all taught and make the learning tools and the lessons as simple and as direct as possible.

Lastly, this book is not about male or female bashing. For the record, men have their share of drama. They are not the best communicators to suit a woman's needs (i.e. listening, romancing, sensitivity etc) and the list goes on and it's a long list. If I were addressing a book on relationships for men I would write the book as straightforward as possible. In order for a man to truly be respected and honored by his woman, it would be in his best interest to be educated on as many subjects as possible. If he wants to be the head of the household, the CEO if you will, he needs to be knowledgeable about relationships, finances, real estate, health, diet, communication, conflict resolution, etc. As the head of the household, his wife and kids should respect him. His wife should feel submissive in his arms, not because she is weak, but because he is strong. He has proven that he is competent and confident to head the household. He should be a great role model for his family. I would get very specific about the responsibilities men have in their relationship.

If a man is not handling his responsibilities, the woman has no choice but to co-chair or be the CEO of the relationship and wear the pants. I don't believe women want to wear the pants in a relationship, but if the man isn't going to fulfill his responsibilities, then she will and should. So this book isn't about taking sides. It is written specifically for women, about chocolate's behavior.

I want to be straightforward and persistent. I want you to get the message loud and clear. I've taught these lessons to many women. I know the lessons work. These are my beliefs, values, and points of view. If at any time during your reading of the book you are offended, I apologize. This book is not about offending women. I want to educate women. I am aware that some of the issues I confront are not written to be politically correct. They are written to be honest or to drive the point home. At times the message is repetitive, again only to instill the importance of the point.

I have been accused of giving tough love when necessary and in the same breath I've been thanked. Recently a friend of mine left me a voice message thanking me for and I quote, "You single handedly saved my life." Referring to what could have been a nasty and costly divorce. I showed her a higher road to take and how to win without using her negative energy (i.e. swearing, threats, and name calling). I also helped her with the choices she is making in her new relationship to understand her man's behavior and stop asking the question, "What does it mean?" It took her a couple of weeks in the beginning to wrap herself around some of these concepts. When she got them, she got them; hence the voice message. My one and only request is that you read this book with an open mind and spirit because that is how this book is written. Allow yourself the emotional and spiritual space for the information to become a part of who you are. You are never given a challenge you cannot handle. If this book is in your hands, welcome to the challenge.

I want to make it very clear that this book is based on generalization. I know there are exceptions to every rule, but generalizations come from somewhere. We live in finite societies and there are only so many choices of colors, shapes, and sizes to choose from. Because of these fixed choices we all fit into a group or generalization. People who drive minivans are generally people with kids or who want kids. Generally speaking, people with less education make less money than those with higher education. Women love to buy shoes and men generally love sports. I want this book to speak to the generalities of relationships and the people in them.

When reading this book it will be easy to let the emotional you overcome the logical you, but keep in mind that this book addresses the generalities of our lives, not the exception. If you are an exception, you probably have a friend, sister, mother, or aunt who is the rule. Enjoy the process and enjoy the book.

Good Luck~

Milk Chocolate ~

Chocolate causes certain endocrine glands to secrete hormones that affect your feelings and behavior by making you happy. Therefore, it counteracts depression, in turn reducing the stress of depression. Your stress-free life helps you maintain a youthful disposition, both physically and mentally. So, eat lots of chocolate!
Elaine Sherman, Book of Divine Indulgences

The Chocolate Relationship

After attending a women's independent filmmakers festival, I found myself at a house party in Hancock Park, (an upper class neighborhood in Los Angeles, California) surrounded by a group of intelligent, creative, sensitive, and interesting professional females. As I waited for my male friends to arrive, I decided to lay low and listen to what these women had to say, considering I am outnumbered 22 to 1.

The conversation among the ladies began with them talking about the festival itself: how well it is organized, the amount of people that attended the event, and how it brought the community of female filmmakers together. As they began talking about their favorite films; intriguingly, they had a unanimous favorite. Much to my surprise, their choice was a film titled *"The Love I Lost,"* which dealt with a woman who couldn't help but to fall in love with a guy who is unable to love her as much as she wanted to be love and as much as she loved him. At this point I truly became enthralled with their tête-à-tête.

The film takes place in Chicago. The female lead character is Mimi, a 5'5"and 110 lbs with long dark brown hair and a cute crooked smile. Mimi has a successful and thriving career as an investment banker at one of the city's largest banks, a real go-getter. She's a University of Chicago undergrad and Northwestern University post grad with an MBA. She has strong moral beliefs, is self reliant, and drug free. On paper she could have anything and any man she wanted. What she wanted is to one day be married to an honorable man and raise a family together. What she got is Jake, 100% pure milk chocolate, whom she is crazy about.

Mimi grew up in a middle class suburban neighborhood just north of Chicago; the oldest of three kids including one sister, one brother, mother and father. Her mother a 1950's June Cleaver type is a school teacher and her dad although a great guy, is a modern day Archie Bunker who has spent the last twenty-eight years as a career pharmaceutical sales representative. As in most American households, her mom is the homemaker, caretaker and nurturer. Her father is the main financial provider and although he is in the household, he is incapable of meeting most of his family's emotional needs. Mimi has never seen her father cry or show much affection towards her mother. He isn't much of a disciplinarian either and keeps his own feelings tucked inside. Much of his time and pleasure is spent traveling for business and he only attends important events in his children's lives like graduations, birthdays, and holidays. Mimi got most of her love and affection in her formative years from her mother and grandparents.

Sadly, Mimi's father avoided talking to her about issues that his daughter would one day need to understand; two of those issues being basic male behavior and sexuality between the sexes. What her father did teach her about men is that, "All men will want from her is sex" and "Men can't be trusted." And in so many words, "Men are dogs." Unbeknownst to her father, he defined Mimi's self-worth as a sexual object for men, which has crippled her in her relationships with men. He neglected to tell her that men have many needs besides sex, such as the need to be nurtured, loved, validated, and appreciate and to give the same in return. He didn't set the best example of the other positive qualities men possess such as leadership, wisdom, spirituality, caring, expression, thoughtfulness, consideration, compassion, humor, affection, playfulness, intelligence, love, courage, and ambition.

Mimi learned at a very early age that in order to receive love and attention from her father she would have to compete with her mother, her siblings, her father's job, and his personal interest in vintage electronics such as old radios. Mimi had a lot to compete with when she wanted and needed his attention and that pattern to compete for love continued in her personal adult relationships.

The male lead character, Jake, is your classic bad boy; typically dressed in tight black jeans, renegade motorcycle boots, studded black leather belt, and his signature 70's rock band concert t-shirts. One of his many tattoos on his right arm in bold blood red and black ink is his mantra, "Go Bigger, or Go

Home" an expression of his over-indulgence. Jake is very charming, handsome, dangerous, creative, self-indulgent, passionate, intelligent, needy, and funny. He frequently uses drugs or other substances. His favorite drink is Jack Daniels with a splash of coke and his favorite drugs are ecstasy and marijuana. However, he lacks the developmental and emotional skills to know how to commit to Mimi or any woman. Jake grew up in a single parent household with no brothers and a half-sister, whom he has yet to meet. His father moved out when he was is in 3rd grade and a year later his parents were divorced. His mother worked two jobs to afford the small two bedroom apartment they shared. Jake's mother did her best to raise him to be a man, as noble as that seems this blunder has unremitting consequences.

Despite the fact that he is the only child, his mother is rarely available for him. She worked long hours and when she is home she drank herself to sleep. He often begged his mother to stop drinking and to participate in his life. She returns his plea for validation with passive-aggressive rejection. Having her own issues with men in general, Jake's mom never gets too close to him, which results in Jake not being able to trust others. His only wall of defense is making others laugh and when he isn't the center of attention, he found his solace writing songs and his guitar. Jake dreams of being a rock star and one day performing in large arenas to screaming fans, but until that day comes he works at Effie's Catering Company as a Sous Chef.

Mimi and Jake met through a mutual friend named Amy who is certain they will be perfect for each other. Amy thought Mimi would loosen up by being with a musician and Jake would have structure in his life by dating a professional business woman, all under the assumption that opposites attract. In the early stages of their relationship it seemed that way, at least for Jake. When they started dating, Mimi was very much like Jake's mother. She worked full time and had an active social life, Mimi isn't always available and she didn't care to see his band perform, it isn't her type of music. The fact that she isn't a groupie made him immediately attracted to Mimi's as well as her beauty and personality.

Mimi is attracted to Jake, but her instincts tell her to proceed with caution. She shies away from Jakes advances. When Jake flatters her with affection she brushes it off. With any gifts, flowers, or gestures of caring Mimi's walls of caution go up. Mimi's rejection actually turns him on and he can't get enough of her. In the back of Mimi's mind she questions his motivation to pursue her with his unconditional attention. She thinks to herself, he barely knows me, so how could he feel so strongly? Subconsciously, he sees the challenge with her as he did with his mother, the trigger to compete for female attention.

One night while sitting in Mimi's new black E-class Mercedes Benz, Jake exposes his vulnerable side and confesses some of his painful childhood experiences. His confessions melt Mimi's heart and she wants to mend his pains. She feels he needs someone like her to love him - she feels needed. Ultimately his charming personality wins her over. What she once rejected, she now accepts with open arms. Trust replaces uncertainty as they spend every waking and resting hour together. She is convinced that she has indeed found true love and happiness. Every day she falls deeper in love and is convinced she is in a committed relationship.

What Mimi loved most about Jake is his passion for music and his sense of humor. He could keep her laughing for hours. By far the funniest man she had ever dated and his knowledge of music is unsurpassed. He can name most songs by listening to only the first five notes. The combination of his intelligence and laughter manifest into incredible mind-blowing sex; Mimi is hooked on chocolate.

Life between them seemed magical: kissing and hugging every chance they got. They have no shame for PDA – *Public Display of Affection*. They are in inseparable. Considering Jake makes a quarter of Mimi's income after taxes, Mimi didn't think twice about buying him a $6500.00 vintage Gibson guitar that was once owned by the legendary Chuck Berry, as a just because gift. She pays for all of their dinner dates, his rent, and bought him a black Dodge Ram truck he always dreamed of owning. Mimi feels this is a small price to pay for happiness, besides "What's the point of having money if you can't share it with the one you love." Eventually Mimi suggests that he move into her Lake Shore Drive condo, an offer that Jake welcomes, but this sends up his flag of caution.

Ironically, shortly after Mimi commits, Jake begins putting up his walls and pushes her away. The paradox is that Jake did everything to get Mimi's attention and acceptance, but he is uncomfortable with the adulation of love and attention that Mimi gives him in return. It is the chase that triggers Jake's relentless motivation to pursue and now that he has her, the challenge is gone and so is most of the excitement for him.

Instead of being honest with Mimi about his feelings, Jake made excuses for spending less and less time with her; he needed more time to practice with his band and he needed to work weekends. The truth is that Jake barely touched his guitar since they started dating and rarely worked at Effie's Catering Company on weekends anymore. Distancing himself from her leads to arguments between them and much emotional confusion for Mimi; nevertheless, the more Jake pulled away the deeper she fell in love and craved his attention.

Mimi didn't understand why he showered her with affection in the first two months of the relationship and then pulled away just as they were getting closer. The best answer Mimi can come up with is to take the blame for not giving him enough. Wanting to see and please him, she buys him one gift after another. One gift is an iPhone so he would stay in contact. This didn't work because Jake never used it and definitely didn't want to be accessible.

Yet when Jake needs sex, he calls her in the middle of the night knowing she has to work the next day. Mimi gladly obliges. Just as her father taught her, "All men want from me is sex," she again has become a sexual object to a man. Sometimes when Jake is in a selfish mood, he would ask to leave right after sex: no cuddling, no hanging around, no dinner just *bam slam thank you ma'm*. When Jake is being a jerk, Mimi's weakness for him overlooks his actions. Being the loving girlfriend, she pathetically understands and makes excuses for his behavior. "Oh musicians are moody because they are creative." Or "I know he loves me, he just need-his space."

Now that Jake has Mimi's heart wrapped around his finger, things between them are never the same. As the months pass the most minuscule incidents trigger an argument between them. Jake balks at how Mimi parks the car, which turns into a three hour fight. Jake argues to push her away, which is his way of sending the message, "The chase is over, I'm bored and I need to find another relationship." Mimi argues and fights so Jake can feel her pain, frustration, and find some connection between them. Regardless of the fighting she wants to send the message that in spite of their differences, she still loves him and is willing to work things out, a message that never makes it to Jake's ears.

Their common interest that held them together, e.g. Blockbuster nights, laughter, sitting cozy on the couch, and PDA, now sets off their venomous fights. Jake prefers not to be seen with Mimi and any display of PDA is a turn off. Jake complains that Mimi eats too much and is too smothering. He says anything to push her away. When fighting and throwing insults doesn't push Mimi away, Jake disappears for days at a time, never calling or returning her emails. Jake is unaware that his non-verbal communication is destroying Mimi's self-esteem; he sees it as par for the course of dating. This isn't the first heart he has broken. The hurt she is experiencing is causing undue stress and frustration. It also leaves her suspicious that Jake is seeing another woman.

As depression gets the best of her, she withdraws from family and friends. She stops returning their calls, and her personal life is pure chaos. Her condo is filthy with laundry everywhere, her sink is stacked with dirty dishes, and her cupboards are empty. Her job performance suffers so much that her boss and colleagues are concerned with her well-being. Her broken heart also affects her physical well-being. Mimi gets frequent migraine headaches, the thought of food makes her nauseous, and she involuntarily loses weight and now weighs 82 pounds.

After weeks or even days apart, it doesn't take long before separation anxiety gets the best of both of them. They miss each other so much it hurts. They miss their addiction to fighting; to them it is disguised as passion. They temporarily bandage this hurt by reuniting to fill each other's emotional emptiness. Once they are temporarily satisfied physically and emotionally (they get their addictive fix) their pattern arguing and separation repeats itself. When Jake sees Mimi he inevitably would ask her for cash. Not directly, he would hint that his cash flow is low and that he needed money for rent, money for rehearsal space, and even money to buy his medical marijuana. Ha ha!

Family and friends observe Mimi's highs and lows and they strongly suggest she get out of her relationship with Jake before it is too late. They tell her to get a man that would appreciate her. They also tell her to get an educated man, a man with stability, and a man who wouldn't be intimidated by her career, income, and beauty. She deserves better. They feared the reckless Jake will impregnate Mimi leaving her to be a single mom, ruining her career and life. They think the love struck Mimi is too blind to take the necessary precautions and that she will have a baby just to trap Jake.

Mimi complains about her relationship issues to everyone, but resents hearing the negative comments about Jake. She often engages in arguments with people closest to her and defends Jake's behavior although she knows there is truth in what they are saying. What Mimi didn't know is how to handle the dynamics of her chocolate. Her options were to: A - accept the situation, B - shut up and stop complaining, or C - move on. She chooses the latter after one of Jake's disappearing acts.

Reluctantly, she takes the advice of friends and family to stop communicating with Jake. All the while, Mimi's heart is broken by the man she loved most. Jake can make her the happiest woman in the world and the saddest all in the same breath.

A week later she doubts their better judgment. She breaks her agreement and calls Jake in the middle of the night and the moment she hears his voice she immediately hangs up. Unsatisfied and yearning for a glimpse of Jake, she drives to his apartment and sits for hours in her car waiting to see him and who is coming in and out of Jake's life all while listening to the love song Jake wrote for her the day they met.

One of Mimi's dilemmas is feeling betrayed by Jake and her family for different reasons; Jake being the obvious, friends and family because they encouraged her to leave her chocolate. To compensate for encouraging the break up, everyone in Mimi's life is playing matchmaker. It doesn't take long for her to be introduced to Robert, the 6'1", handsome all-American man. The matchmaker is none other than her friend Amy, the friend who introduced her to Jake.

Robert is a Duke University undergraduate with an MBA from Georgetown University. He wears Brooks Brother's suits to work and polo IZOD shirts and Dockers for weekend casual wear. He drives a silver 5-series BMW and owns a grey stone in the Lincoln Park District of Chicago's north side. He does not have much of a sense of humor or a fan of pop music. He does enjoy reading the Wall Street Journal, Forbes, and The New York Times. His favorite television shows are Business Nation, MSNBC, and The Big Idea with Donny Deutsch.

On their first date, Robert takes an immediate liking to Mimi and who can blame him. She's beautiful, intelligent, and they had great conversation. Throughout the night he can't keep his eyes off her and flatters her with compliments every chance he gets. Mimi senses his weakness for her and subconsciously begins testing his manhood and how far she could push the boundaries. She calls him Bob when he clearly prefers to be called Robert. Instead of taking a stance and letting Mimi know it is unacceptable for her to call him Bob, he fears rejection and accepts the name change. Something she could never do with Jake. He would put her in her place.

In contrast to Jake, on paper Bob is everything they said she needs in a man to be happy. He's worked as a commercial mortgage broker for the past 12 years. He is reliable, loyal, educated, financially secure, drug-free, and family oriented. He is close to his parents and siblings and one day in the near future wants to be married and have children.

Mimi and Bob begin seeing each other on a regular basis. Although throughout her courtship with Bob, Mimi can't get Jake out of her heart and mind. Bob treats Mimi very well; he calls her at least once a day, and they dine in the best restaurants. He makes special arrangements for her birthday with orchestra seats to attend her favorite musical, *Wicked,* at the Shubert Theater and even planned a vacation he thought she would enjoy. Bob always puts Mimi first.

To repay Bob's thoughtfulness, Mimi would on occasion claim to be tired and need some rest. Often it would happen after an expensive dinner that she would give Bob the perfunctory pat on the back and then race over to see Jake. Being the nice guy he never suspected Mimi of sleeping with Jake or any other man. She rarely spoke of Jake in Bob's presence, although Jake is an intricate part of Mimi's life.

By the fall of that year, Jake is bored with Mimi's submissive behavior. There is no challenge for him; he says "jump" and she says "how high?" Jake has no choice but to completely shut her out of his life. He stops taking her phone calls and sleeping with her. The isolation isn't enough for Mimi to get the message that Jake is no longer interested. The rejection triggers her compulsive impulses to crave more abuse. She begins to live out improbable scenarios in her head of her and Jake getting back together as a couple. These kinds of thoughts only send Mimi into an emotional fury. One night she stands up Bob and misses his important award ceremony where he is being honored as the employee of the year. Mimi never gives Bob's feelings a second thought as she hastens to Jake's apartment unannounced. Dressed in a pair of form fitting True Religion jeans, a sexy Juicy jacket, a Marc Jacobs blue and yellow scarf wrapped around her neck, a Kate Spade purse slung over her shoulder, with her naturally wavy hair flat ironed straight, she arrives at Jake's front door. She wants to make a great impression. Anxiously, she knocks on the door and calls out Jake's name. "Hi Jake – It's me – I got a surprise for you." Mimi reaches into her purse to pull out a wrapped gift for Jake. The front door leisurely opens and Mimi is greeted by Bree, a woman dressed in a sexy outfit and who is just as beautiful if not more beautiful than Mimi. When Bree asks, "Can I help you?" Mimi is speechless and her eyes well up. In the background she hears Jake's voice, "Baby who's at the door?" Devastated and crushed like a grape, Mimi hurries back to her car dropping her scarf and gift box behind. She opens her car door and immediately begins to cry. She manages to turn on the car and slowly drives away. In her rearview mirror she sees Jake with his arm around Bree standing in the doorway and her new scarf lying in the middle of the cold street next to the box. Her car's stereo plays Aretha Franklin's hit song, "I Never Love A Man (The Way I Love You). She listens to every word in the song…

You're a no good heart breaker – You're a lair and you're a cheat – And I don't know why – I let you do these things to me – My friends keep telling me – That you ain't no good – But oh, they don't know – That I'd leave you if I could – I guess I'm uptight – And stuck like glue – Cause I ain't never – I ain't never, I ani't never, no, no love a man – The way that I love you….

Angrily, Mimi takes out her cell phone and toggles through the menu mode searching for Jake's number. She feels she needs to say something to him, if only to vent her frustration. She is an emotional wreck and can't seem to follow the simple steps she has done a thousand times to make a call. Drenched in tears her phone rings, it's the forever thoughtful and considerate Bob calling from the banquet. Bob asks, "Where are you? Why aren't you here?" "Is everything is ok, where you in a car accident?" Holding back her sorrow, she replies, "I'm just not feeling well, I'll call you tomorrow." Bob is not happy Mimi is a no-show, but he has sympathy. Bob says, "If you need anything let me know… I love you." Mimi says, "Me too." Mimi drives home playing Aretha Franklin's song over and over again.

The next morning, Mimi plots to get even with Jake or better yet, to move on with her life, or so she thinks. Mimi convinces herself that she could make things work out between her and

Bob. At the same time, she hopes that Jake would discover her new romance, get jealous, and want her back. None the wiser of her hidden agendas, Bob acquiesces to become more committed to the relationship. Family and friends believe Mimi has finally come to her senses. Mimi wonders to herself if she has changed.

As time passes, Jake and all things associated with him seem to fade. She deletes his name from her phone and discards letters and photos. Bob and Mimi continue spending quality time together shopping, dining, traveling, and socializing. Mimi regains her ideal weight and her work performance is back up to her standards. The outside world sees them as the perfect ideal couple, something friends and family want to emulate.

Bob's feelings grow fast and every day he is more in love than the next. Bob believes her feelings are mutual and that he has found his soul mate! The more time Mimi spends with Bob, she thinks she will grow to love him just the same, but it never happens. Living the good life with Bob, aka Mr. Right drives Mimi to her wits end. The straw that breaks the camel's back comes when Bob gets down on bended knee and asked Mimi for her hand in marriage at half time on center court of a Chicago Bulls basketball game. Being put on the spot in front of thousands of people, Mimi says "Yes." The thought of spending a lifetime with Bob sends shivers up her spine. Later that night over dinner, she gives Bob back the ring and rejects his proposal. She explains he did nothing wrong and that he is a not bad guy, but she never gets butterflies in her stomach when she sees him. The spark never flew and the sex as much as she wanted it to be more, is subpar, due in part to his lack of imagination and passion.

Bob is her mixed-green salad - good for you, but boring compared to chocolate. What Mimi misses in her life is some good rich Belgian milk chocolate - not sugar free, not low calorie. She needs and wants rich, high-in-calories chocolate. The kind of chocolate that just one bite won't do, the kind that will make you get out of bed in the middle of the night for just another taste, and the kind that will makes you cheat on your Jenny Craig diet. That's the kind of chocolate Mimi misses and Bob isn't.

Much to the disappointment of her friends, family, and especially Bob, Mimi ends their relationship. Bob questions his own integrity and character. Speculating that it is the size of his manhood she doesn't like. Should he have been more aggressive? Bob recalls a conversation with Mimi about relationships, where she claimed she wanted a nice, loving, honest, caring, responsible, considerate man with a job and who would be ready to start a family. Bob is all of the above. For the life of him he can't imagine what he did wrong to not win her heart. Little does he know Mimi isn't forthright with him. She always sees him as a boring man to whom she could never fully give herself to. He is her prop to fill time. She used him to make herself feel better; to feel she had some sense of self-worth left. Never ever did Bob dream that while he and Mimi made love, it is Jake whom she moaned for!

Bob is shattered, but this isn't his first heartbreak it's more the story of his life. He asks Mimi out several more times afterwards hoping that she has a change of heart or that she will give him a second chance to do better. Filled with guilt, she grants him one last dinner selfishly to save her own face. In the end, the best she can offer; although, to no consequence to

Bob, is her friendship, which can never be a real friendship because all that they have experienced was a deception.

With no Bob or Jake in her life, she is depressed, lonely, and not feeling that great about herself once again. She betrayed Bob, an honest man, and wants Jake, the jerk. She rejects dating men with any resemblance to a Mr. Nice Guy or to Jake. Her weight shifts as she is eating more calories than she is burning. Those extra pounds only further add to her depression. As summer nears Mimi is back to her old self. Her weight is back to normal and she is spending quality time with family and friends and her career is booming. In spite of all the good in her life, Mimi spends many nights in bed dreaming and wishing for Jake. Mimi wonders what it would take to get him back. Is it a mistake that she let her chocolate get away? What could she have done to keep her chocolate? Would she ever find that type of chocolate ever again? Would he ever call? Mimi mulls over these questions repeatedly.

On a lonely rainy night while sitting in front of her TiVo player watching a week's worth of Dr. Phil and Oprah episodes, her phone rings around midnight. "Hello" – "Hey girl it's me, Jake!" "Yeah, what are you doing?" "Nothing... I mean watching TV." Mimi is thrilled to hear Jake's voice. Jake invites Mimi over to his house across town. "Come over I want to see you." For a moment Mimi is level headed, then said, "Jake where have you been? Why should I drive through town to see you and why are you calling me out of blue?" Jake simply replies, "I wanted you, do you want to see me or not?" Mimi's emotions kicked in; she thinks that's so sweet he missed her. She replies "You do?" Jake – "Yeah, I got your scarf." Mimi's eyes begin to tear up. No faster than she could hang the phone up, Mimi hurries out of bed, showers-exfoliating every inch of her body, shaves her legs smooth, and slips on a mini skirt with no panties and pumps. She takes one last look in the full length mirror to check how much skin is showing; just enough to tease him. Then she dashes out the door and quickly drives across town to the chocolate she missed and loves so much… The End

Chocolate Truffles ~

"Nobody knows the truffles I've seen!" *Anonymous*

We Like What We Like

The women from the film festival all related to Mimi and Jake's relationship in one way or another, based on their own relationship experience. Some thought she should have walked away from Jake and get a man that really cared about her, if not Bob then another guy, and if not that guy then the next. A woman should keep searching until she finds what she is looking for and not settle. Why should she? Some made excuses for Mimi to stay in that relationship, i.e. Jake does make an effort at times, it's not his fault, his mother is the culprit, or it's not his mother's fault, blame the dad. Others thought that if Mimi and Jake got some couples counseling they would stay together. Most saw Jake as a lost soul who needed Mimi's love and attention; he could and would eventually change, with a woman's help.

Whether any of us consider the relationship between Mimi and Jake healthy or not, we all would agree, like Mimi, that we all like what we like. Whether it's a pair of Manolo Blahnik shoes, Marc Jacob's scarf, a Kate Spade purse, cheesecake for dessert or a Hawaii vacation, we make choices based on what we desire or feel is in our best interests - that will never change. If you like chocolate you are going to buy chocolate, if you buy chocolate you are surely going to eat chocolate, and that is the truth of the matter.

Mimi is attracted to Jake because he behaves as chocolate does; he's unpredictable, creative, charming, exciting, edgy, and fascinating. There is nothing wrong with those qualities. The hitch is that Mimi has a difficult time comprehending that chocolate will never behave as salad does. Mimi's inability to see this dichotomy is the source of her relationship conflict. Even if she could change her chocolate and discipline it to behave like salad she wouldn't know where to begin. She was never taught by her parents how to manage herself, her relationships, or how to behave as a worthy partner in a relationship.

Conflicts will always exist when you don't understand how to manage your likes and desires; this is not only true with love, but also in many aspects of our lives. We live in a compulsive, addictive, and overly indulgent society, seemly with no control over our behavior. Observe how many people in this country are overweight, maxed out on credit card debt, hooked on tobacco, or addicted to drugs or alcohol. People love food but can't manage their portions, control their desire for unhealthy food, nor can they stick to a healthy diet. Like Mimi, ironically, they expect a different result than what they get, which is weight gain, in the case of food.

Who takes the time to study the side effects of sugar? How many people can go to a bar, have just one drink, and avoid wandering home drunk? How many people smoke marijuana on a daily basis and then question why they are not top performers? How many people start their day with a cup of coffee or cigarette and expect no side effects? Millions! In this case, Jake is the same as drugs and alcohol. Since you are going to indulge in these pleasures, you owe it to yourself to at least learn how much is too much. Learn about the chemicals in your food and the side effects. Mimi is not prepared to be in a relationship, especially with someone like Jake and has to accept the results she gets, just as a person who doesn't know the difference between junk food and health food. They too have to accept the results they eventually get, unless they educate and discipline themselves.

In most areas of your life you are ready and prepared. You go to college to prepare for a job. Before you buy a computer, car, or a house, you shop around and compare prices. You ask the experts questions in their given field to help you make the right choice. You don't ask a car salesman questions about real estate. You don't ask a bank teller about cars. You pay your debt to keep your credit in good standing so that you are prepared to make a major purchase one day. You should have the same tenacity and preparedness in your relationship. Do your homework and don't just learn by life experiences. You wouldn't want to buy ten houses or ten cars before you finally get a good deal? Do your due diligence. As much as love is a feeling it is also a responsibility and business.

When Jake behaves as chocolate does, Mimi loves it. She loves the charge and the excitement she gets from her Jake. On the other hand, she is frustrated and disappointed. She complains about her relationship to friends and family. They in turn insist that she abandon the chocolate she so desires. Those questioning her integrity and choices are themselves just as attracted, have been attracted, or addicted to the chocolate of their choice; although, some people around her have given up and accepted salad.

With a few exceptions, we make choices based on our likes and dislikes. Even when it comes down to making choices based on what is good for us versus what is in our best interest, we generally choose what we enjoy. A woman buys a pair of Gucci shoes based on what she finds appealing about the shoes, not based on how good the shoes are constructed or the health benefits for her feet. In some instances, a woman will skip meals to save money to purchase a pair of shoes, a purse, or an outfit, regardless of price and sacrifice to her well-being. Eating *Top Ramen* noodles probably doesn't fulfill all of your nutritional needs, but for some women it's worth the sacrifice. All because she likes what she likes and wants to have the shoes at any cost. Her shoes are her chocolate at that moment. This is also true for our choice of cars, clothes, friends, close relationships, and our entertainment. The shoes may hurt, but you've just got to have them. Yes, some of us do eat healthy foods, date the ideal person, but those things are also based on our likes and dislikes. Be okay with what you like. Understand that the people who might be judging you about the choices you are making are also making choices based on what they like, be it a friend, lover, husband, or wife. Therefore, who are any of us to judge what others like?

If we were to make choices based only on what is really good for us at the core of our being, we would probably find our lives very boring. We wouldn't wear designer clothes, consume alcohol, eat sweets, eat fatty foods, watch *Pretty Woman*, or wear diamonds. We would drive hybrid automobiles, live in affordable green housing, watch the *Discovery Channel*, and date the Mr. and Mrs. Rights of the world, whoever they are. How boring would that be? As much as we suggest to others to stop eating sweets, exercise more, and stop dating bad boys, and save money, it isn't going to happen. We don't make these choices for ourselves and yet we are judgmental of others! How ironic. Our desires are never going to change, nor do any of us generally advocate change to modify our desires to satisfy others.

When you choose footwear no one ever tells you not to buy Jimmy Choos to settle for Doc Martins, or to settle for just a salad when you are at a French restaurant. Only in our personal relationships with the chocolate we desire, that love or lust can't seem to exist without friends, family, and acquaintances suggesting what is in our best interests. None of them ever really accept the fact that we are attracted to the chocolate of our choice, for our own reasons and are okay with it. I understand that your friends are looking out for your best interest and they don't want to see you hurt or abused. Your girlfriend tells you that the man you are dating is a jerk. "You can do better," she says. Your brother heard little tidbits about the chocolate you are dating and he is ready to break his legs. Your mom is setting you up on a blind date with a guy she believes is better for you than the man you have. No one accepts your choice and more importantly no one is helping you and giving you solid relationship advice. "Dump him", "You can do better" and "He is an A-hole" is not good advice. No one insists you take off your shoes that are pinching your feet because they are made for looks not comfort! Has anyone ever told you "Take off those shoes, you can do better?" Has anyone ever said, "I have a great pair of shoes and you are going to love them. They fit great and are good for you?" No.

Our behavior is driven by our wants and needs to such an extent that the following is a great example of how true this is.

Watching the ABC news program *20/20*, I saw a story titled *The Myths and Truths about Health*. One of the myths explored was, do cosmetic products that claim to get rid of facial wrinkles really work? The *20/20* correspondent interviewed a well-known and respected thirty-something attractive female New York City dermatologist. They asked her whether it is a myth or a truth that cosmetic companies do have creams to eliminate facial wrinkles. After examining many samples, the dermatologist said that based on her experience and research she found it to be a myth. There is no scientific evidence that proves conclusively that a particular cream, ointment, or lotion permanently removes wrinkles. Then the correspondent of that *20/20* segment asked the dermatologist if she had ever bought over the counter wrinkle creams at a department store with the hope they would remove her age lines. The dermatologist, who only a few minutes earlier had said there is no scientific evidence that any of the creams work, paused for a minute and said yes she, had bought wrinkle creams to combat her own wrinkles.

This intelligent woman who treats skin every day, a woman who has heard of every concoction to remove wrinkles, knew the scientific proof that potions and lotions don't work. Still she bought wrinkle products for her skin. Is she doing what is in her best interest, or buying the wrinkle products because she likes them? She purchased wrinkle removers based on her likes, her needs and her desires, just as a woman will buy a pair of shoes based on her likes and not what is in her best interest for her feet. It's also the same way she chooses her chocolate. This is also how we choose relationships based on what we like and on what make us feel good. There are many reasons we like something or someone, but, nevertheless, it's all based on what we like.

Chocolate is not the culprit in your life. When you indulge in chocolate it is because it's what you like. All you have to do is understand the rules of chocolate. Chocolate has its own set of rules that are different from that of salad. In contrast to a green salad, if you eat too much chocolate, as Mimi did, you can get a heart-ache or a belly-ache. You can gain weight and break out in pimples. If you learn the properties of chocolate and are aware of how chocolate behaves you can manage your chocolate craving and not gain excessive weight and also avoid heart-ache. You will know when to take a bite, how much you can chew, and which chocolate to get involved with.

Observation

We are taught that love is something that is just supposed to happen. The unfortunate truth is that you go through life dating many men and doing your best. Then you figure out one way or another that love isn't something that just happens. Relationships take work on oneself and as a partnership. Unfortunately, the only consistent tool or advice most women are given about men is that all men want from women is sex, that men can't be trusted, and that they are cheaters. Parents revel in that litany as if that is all a woman needs to prepare for her future relationships. Not only is the advice shallow and ignorant, it also leaves her unarmed for what is to come. Even worse it contributes to her sense of self-worth when she is told that all men want from women is sex and that men can't be trusted. Do such men include males she loves and admires such as her grandfather, father, or brother?

Young girls are taught by the media, schools, parents, and Church, that they are going to meet Mr. Right. They are to marry, have kids, live in a house with a picket fence, and live happily ever after. They say this as if we live in two separate worlds, one for the Mr. Rights and the other for cheaters and the un-trustworthy. Commercials, movies, romance novels, talk shows, friends and family all promote the perfect image of love, which leads her to believe that any couple that is holding hands and cuddling have a prefect relationship. Any of us will compare ourselves to those images on television and say, "I want that relationship." The happy couple in the park represents to us what love is, what happiness is, and what we should strive for in a relationship. These images even make us think our relationship failed because we are unlucky and got stuck with the cheating loser. These are only ideals and images sold to you to change your idea or perception about a product or ideal. It is not the reality. I'm not saying that couples don't fall in love and live happily ever after, generally speaking, it's the exception, not the rule to have such a perfect relationship. The truth is that we don't know about those couples - did they just meet? Are they making up? Who knows?

Another example of this is when a woman asks a man, "How did you meet your girlfriend?" He tells her they met on a blind date. Immediately she internalizes his experience and says, "They (blind dates) do work," believing that there is hope for her. Little does she know that blind dating, online dating or finding love by chance all take the same amount of effort for a relationship to be a success. She is left to believe that she is missing the magic moment or the moment missed her. She is forever optimistic and believes one day her Mr. Right will arrive.

When you buy into these ideas you are setting yourself up for failure. Because the media promotes the idea that chocolate is behaving just as salad would. You want your Jake to confess his love for you at the end of your dinner date just like a scene out of a romantic movie. It never happens, but you are determined to find your Mr. Right. You are not going to settle. You deserve better. These feelings and thoughts are the premise for Hollywood hit movies such as *Pretty Woman, Four Weddings and a Funeral, Sleepless in Seattle, When Harry Met Sally,* and *Jerry Maguire.* Even the television show *The Bachelor* sells the idea that chocolate can and will behave like salad.

It leads you to believe that: 1) Loves just happens, 2) You are going to find "The One", your soul mate. 3) That your Mr. Right is just around the corner and 4) You are going to meet the man of your dreams by chance on a flight from Los Angeles to Paris. These dreams only reinforce your fairytale beliefs and as a result, you are disappointed and are never quite sure why "they" have found their Mr. Right and you are stuck at home alone, or with Mr. Wrong.

Watching our favorite actor on television walk the red carpet at an Awards show, a celebrity interview with Barbara Walters, or watching your favorite actor on the Oprah show, doesn't help your beliefs either. It merely reinforces your quest for "The One." This is not to say that you shouldn't enjoy those programs or let your imagination run wild. It is entertainment, so be entertained. Don't let your reality become warped because it doesn't conform to TV land.

You listen to celebrities talk about how great their chocolate tastes, how considerate their chocolate is, how much they love their chocolate, the amazing honeymoons they take and all because their chocolate is romantic and thoughtful, unlike your chocolate, Jake. So you admire and envy them from a far because they never seem to get the pimples you have. If they do get them, they seem to recover immediately. Jennifer Aniston recovered pretty fast after her break up with Brad Pitt. Jennifer Lopez and Jessica Simpson recovered fast after their break up's.

We all see these images and say to ourselves, "I want my own chocolate," or "I want my chocolate to behave like that guy on television or in that magazine." You watch your girlfriends and their chocolate and you envy them. No one seems to be getting cavities from chocolate except you and when you lose your chocolate or long for chocolate, it's a slow burn. Celebrities and your friends all have their share of up's and downs just as you and I do.

Don't buy into those images and tabloid tales. Everyone gets pimples, and I'll explain why later. You are not alone. In most cases when it comes to love stories, you are getting half the story, half the truth. Granted some women manage their chocolate better than others. Some women have higher or lower tolerance for their chocolate or they are indifferent. Some wouldn't have their chocolate any less than Jake. But rest assured, you are not alone, as most women don't understand chocolate and certainly can't manage it.

No matter how much attention Bob, and other salads of the world, give you, they simply bore you. In general, they lack lust and passion, while with just a small bite of chocolate you're hooked. Then you spend your dating life confused and frustrated because your relationship doesn't make sense. All you want is to love your chocolate; you want to give yourself to him and probably will do anything for him. When you do give yourself, chocolate leaves your heart broken or disappoints you. You want your rich high-in-calorie chocolate to behave like a salad and it is never going to happen. Salad will never have the excitement of chocolate and chocolate will never be as sensible as salad. *But, isn't that why you like chocolate?*

The first step in managing your chocolate is to accept the fact that you like what you like. Be okay with it because everyone likes what they like. When you are in a relationship with your Jake you don't have to take advice from others or punish yourself because you have an attraction to a man others don't agree with. Learn how to manage yourself and your chocolate. In doing so, you'll be making the best decision for yourself and doing what is in your best interest.

Dark & White Chocolate ~

"I don't understand why so many 'so called' chocolate lovers complain about the calories in chocolate, when all true chocoholics know that it is a vegetable. It comes from the cocoa bean, beans are veggies, 'nuff said." Anonymous

Why We Like Whom We Like

BLACK BOX - WHITE BOX THEORY - Mimi and Jake's relationship similar to most relationships in the world is based on the *Black Box - White Box Theory*. There are three levels to the black box - white box theory, and each has its own rules and values. In each of the levels, you are either the black box, the white box, or you are the white box and he is black box. It doesn't matter which box you are, as you'll see.

Level 3 (Salad / Mr. Nice Guy) is the most humble and modest relationship level. The black and white boxes don't move. They are stagnant throughout the life of the relationship. The **Level 2** (Chocolate / Jake) is the most common type of relationship, which is high in passion, fear, pain, and uncertainty (e.g. Mimi and Jake). In a **level 2** relationship, the boxes are always in motion; one box is always chasing the other. **Level 1** (A little Chocolate, a little Salad on the side) a combination of both - is the most desired relationship and the most difficult to achieve. It is based on honor, trust and commitment.

<u>**LEVEL 3**</u> - The two boxes are separate of each other respectively. In a **level 3** relationship, the boxes are stagnant. There is no chase. The relationship is dull, inactive and lacks

passion. The rules of this relationship are that you don't rock the boat, you don't ask for your needs to be met, and you don't make waves. A recognizable **level 3** relationship may be your uncle and his wife, your grandparents, or a neighbor. They are the couples who have been together for years, but you have never seen them kiss or show passion toward one another. The man has been working the same job for the past forty years and the wife stays home. The woman has the same hairstyle for years and the house has the same furniture for years.

This relationship is apathetic and the couple accepts life as. It's routine and by most standards it's uninteresting. Another common **level 3** relationship is that of a woman who lived most of her adult life in a **level 2** relationship (Chocolate / Jake). Then, one day when the pain of heartbreak and disappointment from her chocolate is too much, she eventually conforms for the **level 3** relationship. She dates or marries the guy that has been hanging around for years and has always been there for her. The same guy she never gave a second thought to or simply only considered him "friend" material - the understudy. Another scenario is as follows: she is in her thirties-forties and the biological clock is ticking so she modifies her needs and conforms to the guy (salad) who will be a great provider for the family and give her the financial security she wants. Nevertheless, inside her raw lust for chocolate remains.

I'm not knocking her decision. I get it - she wants children and security. You should always go after what you want. She gets what she wants and the understudy finally gets the girl whom he has been listening to talk about the chocolate she has been enjoying for years. He believes she has finally come to her senses and his Mr. Nice Guy / Mr. Sensitive persona has finally paid off. He will never know she will crave the bad boy the way she craves chocolate for the rest of their lives together. He'll never know about some of the freakiest things she has done or has fantasized about.

Christy, who is in her early thirties, would invite me over to her house every now and then. The majority of the conversations were about a guy (i.e. chocolate) that she is dating. Come to think of it, she only invited me over when she was in a relationship and wanted me as her sounding board. Nonetheless, all the guys she is attracted to were like Jake. No matter what I said to her, she loved her truffles, milk chocolate, dark chocolate, and assorted chocolate. The more emotionally unavailable they were to her, the greater her sweet tooth. As she aged, she became less attractive to most men and is very aware of it. The frequent invitations to dinners and parties diminished over time. Even so, the Mr. Nice Guys continued to pursue her with expensive dinners, gifts, or vacations. In her past, Mr. Nice Guy would wine and dine her seven days a week and then afterward she would call her chocolate over for dessert. Now her options were mostly the nice guys (salad), who seem to prey on the once hotties of the world.

Having focused most of her time on chocolate, and not nearly enough time on her career, money became tight for Christy. Earning a waitress income and living beyond her means, she is stuck between a rock and a hard place. Her last piece of chocolate made surf boards in Venice Beach, California for a living and he could barely make ends meet for him, let alone help her. Her surfer boy was a stud: handsome, strong, and is notorious for having a large appetite for blonde Barbies, which frustrated Christy.

About two years ago during one of our talks, she broke down and cried. She said she is tired of being hurt and struggling financially. About a week later she called me and said she had met an amazing guy. I thought to myself, "more chocolate." Not this time. She got herself a, green salad, a computer geek, about 5'8", 185 lbs, with a lot of money. Before I knew it, he moved in with her. I asked her why he moved in and why so soon. She said, "Well we are going to share the rent." I replied, "You mean he is going to pay the rent." She giggled. A year later they were married. He bought her a new Mercedes Benz and a house in the Hollywood Hills. On my many visits since then, I've yet to see them have a passionate moment and she is definitely a passionate person. They have become a **level 3** couple. She doesn't complain and neither does he. He finally got the hot chick and she got the financial and emotional security that she had been longing for. She wouldn't have given the 5"8" 185 lb geek the time of day fifteen years ago.

LEVEL 1

In a **level 1** relationship, the boxes move within centimeters of each other.

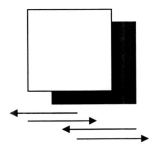

The rules of **level 1** are based on trust, honesty, commitment, and honor. Because this is an honorable relationship, the chase between the two is limited, to say the least, and in most cases, unnecessary because there is mutual respect. It is rare to find this relationship with the opposite sex, other than a family member or best friend. This level by definition is the relationship between a parent and child, sibling, best friends, teammates or comrades; generally found in non-sexual relationships. Although, this is the relationship we all strive to have.

If you are a parent or a pet owner, you've experienced a **level 1** relationship. In both cases, love is equally requited; this is a **level 1** experience. In a **level 3**, love is suspended indefinitely; in a **level 2** relationship love is not equally and mutually reciprocated. Your relationship is in a constant state of uncertainty. To find two people in a **level 1** relationship is unusual, but not impossible.

When you are in a relationship with someone for which you have strong feelings, inevitably your spiritual side, the part of you that unconditionally loves your child, your parents, your best friend or your pets, surfaces. The spiritual you, is different from your physical you. The physical you is the one that has been conditioned by your parents, schools, the church, the neighbors, etc. As a result of your physical conditioning, you are insecure and have self-esteem issues. Let the truth be told, we all have self-esteem issues and insecurities no one is exempt.

When the spiritual you enters into a physical relationship you want to love your partner wholeheartedly and unconditionally, much the same way we love a child; no games, no pretense, just pure love from your soul. The conflict in loving the other person is that we are all prey to physical conditioning. So no matter whom you choose to love they will have self-esteem issues, which will prevent them from loving you wholeheartedly. When you seek to give all the love inside you, you will ultimately be pushed away the same way Jake rejected Mimi because of his self-esteem issues. When your man reciprocates pure love to you, you will sooner or later push him away because of your self-esteem I'll explain the reasons why later.

Your spiritual self thinks, "I just want to love him and not play games." Why is it so hard and frustrating to love someone unconditionally? You are right. It is difficult because the spiritual (**level 1**) has infinite amounts of love to give and at the purest level of loving there are no games. Since we are a product of **level 2** conditioning, those of you who don't want to play games and just want to love your men unconditionally won't be able to, at least not after the first sixty days of being together. When the spiritual you (**level 1**) attempts to love the physical him (**level 2**) it's not going to work because he has all the typical negative social conditioning. Have you ever loved a guy with all of your heart, then one day he returns your love and you lose interest and the challenge is over? Generally, none of us are comfortable with an overwhelming amount of attention or unconditional worship. Due to our conditioning, we need and want the challenge. We prefer to chase than to be chased. The greater the challenge the deeper our spiritual self wants to give love unconditionally. Although the spiritual you wants to love with all of your heart, which is at the **level 1** plane, it is difficult because two people truly have to be on the same level. Beware when the spiritual you is giving love to a physical conditioned person. The relationship will have turmoil because **level 1** and **level 2** values are conflicting.

LEVEL 2

Level 2 - This book focuses mostly on the **level 2** relationship because 98% of the modern world's population is **level 2** individuals. I believe most self-help books and therapies are intended for and attract **level 2** people. If you are in a **level 3** relationship, you probably won't be reading this or any other book on relationships. You wouldn't want to rock the boat. A **level 1** relationship probably doesn't need a book like this. People in a true **level 1** relationship are operating at a mutual honesty level with each other. **Level 1** people were either raised with healthier influences than most, or both people have done the necessary self-help work on their own. Don't feel bad because your relationship is not a **level 1**. Besides, the feeling of being happy is defined by each individual definition of what happiness is. Because happiness is relative, not everyone needs to be in a **level 1** relationship to be satisfied. You can be in any level and experience happiness. You don't have to strive to be in a **level 1** relationship.

The rules for **level 2** are based on fear, uncertainty, lies, disloyalty, insecurity, and unfaithfulness. Negative words and actions are associated with this relationship. Surprisingly, these negative words bring a great deal of excitement to relationship. The boxes in this level are in continuous motion. At any given moment, the boxes can switch from black chasing white, to white chasing black, and back again, all in a single heartbeat.

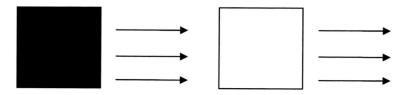

For example, for the past year your guy has been relentlessly chasing you. He calls you, but you don't call back. You have an "I don't care" attitude. Your uncaring attitude makes him chase you even more. Then one day you see him having an intimate conversation with another woman, the physical you panics and your insecurities surface. You live in your head and start playing out scenarios of what your guy is up to. You can't help yourself and you confront him. At this point, he interprets your concerns as neediness. He pulls away. As he pulls away, your insecurities want to grab hold as it becomes more apparent how insecure you really are. The more you pull the more he runs away.

Conflicting Values

Most people have conflicting values on one subject or another. It can be food, money, sexuality, the law, or love. For instance, a person might believe that money is good and serves the greater good. They believe money can provide a better lifestyle for their family and make their lives more comfortable. Their opposing or conflicting value is that money is the root of all evil: crime, war, pain, and suffering are the results of money. Others believe that it's lonely at the top or wealthy people are jerks. Their values about money clash with each another. If you have conflicting values, one value will overcome the other. If your goal is to be rich because you feel it would serve the greater good, the moment you come close to achieving your goal, your opposing value that money is bad emerges. You will subconsciously sabotage your opportunity once you feel you've reached your goal of what you consider rich. You see these opposing value issues with professional athletes or entertainers. For example, a guy, who has a promising career, blows it on a night of drunken disobedience. Another example – chocolate, like Jake, blows the opportunity with a wonderful woman like Mimi, because somewhere in his belief system he thinks he doesn't deserve her.

These conflicting values are definite characteristics of **level 2** relationships. Most people want a **level 1** relationship. They say they want a mate who is honest, committed and loyal. Yet, once they enter a **level 1** relationship, they sabotage it because of their conflicting values. They make excuses as to why they are not happy in the relationship; they are bored, he doesn't dress hip enough, they don't like his friends, etc. The truth of the matter is that their opposing values and regarding why they don't deserve such an honorable person in their life or why such an honorable person would want to be with them rears its ugly head. These are examples of negative values that prevent us from having positive **level 1** relationships.

If being with a **level 1** person bores you because of their honesty, loyalty, and certainty, you will end that relationship and you'll start another one, this time with an exciting **level 2** person. The **level 2** person will eventually cause you too much pain and uncertainty (i.e. Jake). You'll end that relationship with your chocolate and look for Bob (salad). When you are bored with Bob you need excitement and find new chocolate. And the cycle repeats itself over and over. If you continue this cycle to or past the ripe age of thirty-five, you will remain very single and declaring that a good man is hard to find or that you are waiting for your soul mate, aka Mr. Right. It is my belief that between the ages of twenty and thirty-five you have to had met some really good men and for whatever your reasons you sabotage your best chances.

Because **level 2** is so common and we are all attracted to this level relationship, we have to learn how to manage it. Remember, you like what you like. If you like chocolate, eat chocolate. But know the rules of chocolate. It can cause pimples, you can lose your appetite, and it can be an aphrodisiac.

Some women that I have spoken with complain that in order to follow the rules, they feel they're playing a game. All they want to do is love the man they desire. As I mentioned earlier, who we are spiritually makes us want to love another as freely as we like, but it does not work because of our social psycho-osmosis conditioning. Social psycho—osmosis is how we are influenced and absorb information through our social inter-activities - school, home, church and other social circles.

Because we live our lives in the physical self with all the conditioning that comes with it, we all play a game of sorts in most of our adult activities. Your work / professional life doesn't necessarily agree with your personal beliefs, but you don't go to work and tell your boss what you really think of him or her and about the company because you would be fired. You put on your game face and go to work. You drive your car according to the rule of the road. It is no different than playing by the rules in the game of love! The person you are attracted to is just as much a product of physical conditioning as you. Intentionally or unintentionally, he will play games or a game of sorts because he doesn't know any different.

People who say they don't want to play games and just want to love are the very same people who want and need a challenge in their relationships. They wouldn't want someone to just overload them with love and all-consuming attention. They too like and need the chase and are the first to run when they receive the love they claim they need and want to give.

The values that make us feel that we deserve or don't deserve love are inherited values. Your parents passed on their values to you, which they learned from their parents, and so on. You are also taught values by your school teachers, relatives, and friends, which they learned from their predecessors. You also inherit values from organized religion. As if that is not enough influence in shaping one's values, you also have the media. Most of us start watching television and films at an early age, which equals to countless hours of television programming that you absorb during your formative years. This is a tremendous amount of influence, conditioning, and planting of emotional triggers, many of which conflict with the spiritual you wanting to give love unconditionally. To believe your physical values are your own is clearly not true; they are inherited. If these values are not inherently yours, they were taught to you. The irony is that you can be taught new, more effective and empowering values, which is the goal of this book.

Most Common Relationship

Why is a **level 2** relationship the most common in the world? This is the most important question and point in this book. If you understand the answers, you'll discover why you are attracted to chocolate and why your lust for chocolate is so great and deeply rooted. You'll also understand why you are chocolate to some men.

What happens in formative years determines what relationship level a child will most likely respond. The things that we are most attracted to are based on triggers that have been planted and defined in our life. A childhood trigger might be that the color blue relaxes you because as a child your mother bathed you in a blue bathroom with a blue tub and sang to you. Perhaps the smell of pancakes in the morning makes you feel connected because as a child when you had pancakes your parents and grandparents were happily together. A strong trigger for me is driving through a neighborhood in the evening during the prime-time hours (7 to 9PM). If I see television lights flicking through a window, I immediately want to be home to feel connected. That trigger reminds me of being kid, eating popcorn, and watching television with my mother and two brothers.

These triggers begin when you are born. Your parents begin placing triggers in your internal hard drive, which will last a life time. Triggers are set off throughout the day and conjure something different in each of us. It is how we define and shape our existence. Triggers let us know when we are satisfied and dissatisfied and when our needs are met or unfulfilled. When it comes to matters of the heart, we conjure triggers of love and chemistry.

The Family

Very specific events take place in your childhood that make you very, very attracted to chocolate. This phenomenon is prevalent and is worldwide. It happens with the rich, the poor, Blacks, Whites, the sophisticated, and the uneducated. I personally have never met anyone who isn't a product of this childhood **level 2** conditioning. I am not blaming parents for how they raise their children, it is what it is. I truly believe that we all do the best we can do. If we knew more, we would do more. Having said that, I want to give you the best case scenario of an average American family and how the parents with all the best of intention, condition their daughter to develop into a **level 2** person.

In this best case family scenario the father is the breadwinner and works a forty-hour week. The mother is a stay-at-home mom / homemaker involved in the PTA, the community, the church organizations, and other events. They have one child, a 14-year-old daughter.

Let's call this best case scenario family the Robertson's: Daniel the father, Nicole the mother, and their daughter Julie. The Robertson's are your traditional American family with all the challenges that come with life in America. On a typical day in the Robertson household, Julie comes home from school around 3pm, perhaps a little hungry and tired from over stimulation from school and friends. Being a typical 14-year-old girl, school, friends, and guys may not be going as well as she wants. Maybe she is jealous of another female classmate or likes a boy who doesn't like her. Julie could also be feeling the pain of peer pressure (i.e. smoking, sex, and drugs.) Given the reality of puberty, she would ideally like to talk with her parents about her growing pains, even though being a classic male her father is not the greatest listener.

When Julie comes home from school she would like to spend time with Mom and vent about her day. Mom loves her daughter and sincerely wants the best for her, but mom wants to get dinner ready for dad and doesn't have time to chat it up with Julie. As a consolation she makes Julie a snack to hold her over until dinner. Mom and Julie have as much of an intimate conversation as possible between them during the time it takes to make a turkey sandwich. Mom does her best to be a great parent, but hurries Julie off to her room to do homework. She only has a few hours to get dinner ready.

Lately, mom doesn't feel as sexy and attractive as she has in the past. She's a little older and now her daughter is the new symbol of beauty and youth in their household. Mom is also stressed from being involved in too many extra-curricular activities outside the house. Given the fact that she doesn't work and has eight free hours a day, mom needs something to keep her active. Her husband Daniel is a great guy, but lately she doesn't feel connected. She doesn't know why. Is it her, him, or the toll of being married for twenty years? Dad is a good guy and wants to see his family happy. When he comes home from work, he is a little stressed. His company is downsizing and he is now doing the job of two people. The new project manager at work is annoying him. Until the freeway is repaired, the drive to work is adding an extra hour to his commute to and from work. Being a typical guy who loves sports, he is disappointed because his favorite sports team is having a losing season. When dad comes home, he wants and needs some down time to unwind, shuffle through the mail, and have a moment to himself.

At approximately 5:30pm Julie hears her dad's car pull up in the driveway. She runs downstairs and greets him at the door. "Daddy, daddy guess what happened today?" Without waiting a beat or waiting for his reply she continues at the speed of light, "I think I'm going to try out for the cheerleading team, with my friends Holly and Stacy. You know Holly's mom was a cheerleader a long time ago. She is really cute. I saw a picture of her at Holly's house. Stacy said if we make the team all the guys will like us. We'll be so popular. Oh my god, do you think I'm too fat to be a cheerleader? I overheard some girls in the cafeteria call me fat...." Dad says, "No baby you are not fat." Dad wants to put his brief case down... "Daddy... I'm going to need money for my uniform... Dad can I have some money?" Mom – "Honey is that you? Dinner will be ready in a few minutes." "...Daddy what about the money?" "Baby I can't talk about it right now, ask your mother." Dad manages to put his briefcase and belongings down and grab a moment of silence. Julie runs back upstairs and Mom makes the last call that dinner is on the table. "Honey, please wash your hands and get ready for supper!" "I'll be right there."

The Robertson family is seated around the table and enjoying mom's home cooking. Over dinner Julie's parents discuss the necessary family issues, such as the fundraiser for Julie's school, refinancing the house, the cost of cheerleading, and the family vacation. The evening continues on with minimal attention given to Julie. As usual, Dad has sensory overload. Little time is spent on Julie's concerns. When she does speak up to get a word in, Mom usually overrides the conversation to get dad's attention. To pacify Julie, Dad agrees to whatever amount of money she needs for her cheerleading uniform or whatever her other interests are. Instead of a long drawn out discussion over family issues, Dad would rather yield to mom and Julie's demands.

Dad loves his family and likes spending time with them, but he sure would love to sit in front of the television and see if his favorite team can turn their losing season around. Neither parent realizes that Julie has a strong need for undivided attention. After dinner Dad makes a few phone calls, checks his email, and finally catches the last quarter of the game. By now Julie is back in her room on the phone and Mom is doing her best to have an intimate conversation with her husband between the commercials.

This is the way it's been in the Robertson household ever since Julie was born. Dad is usually busy or a non-participant in Julie's activities. It is not that he doesn't care, but it is easier to pass his responsibility of giving her undivided attention to Mom. Mom, being a super mom and nurturer, welcomes the challenge to play the roles of mother and father to Julie. Dad believes a man's role is to provide, while the woman raise the children. He never considers the role he plays in her life as her first relationship with a male. He doesn't realize that he is setting the tone of her values and triggers and that are going to affect her future relationships with men.

When Julie is eighteen years old and leaves the nest what will she have learned about love between a man and a woman? One of the most influential lessons she learns is that love is a need and a want that you *compete for*, à la Mimi. She learns to compete for love and attention. Her dad is essentially too busy or emotionally unavailable. He has taught her to compete against his personal interests, work, television, sports, friends, hobbies, and Mom for his attention. On any given night, Julie gets an average of fifteen minutes combined of undivided attention from both parents. Two minutes here, a minute there, another three minutes while washing the dishes, five minutes at dinner, and so on. She gets attention, but neither parent is really listening or participating at an intimate personal level, especially her father. Her father doesn't have a clue what her favorite color is, her favorite season, her favorite time of day, or what makes her happy or sad. To know these answers he would have to participate with her on an intimate emotional level every day. If he participated at this level, he would be giving her the undivided attention she needs. Knowing these types of answers from the time she is born, he would be setting the trigger that love is a need *that is emotionally and readily available*. It is most important that Julie feels she is a priority.

Unfortunately, the majority of fathers are not emotionally available, or even worse, in some families the father is absent. This conditioning leads to only one result, a young innocent girl born a **level 1** child transformed into a **level 2** woman, who will be attracted to the chocolate and chase her future intimate relationships. By default she is going to be most attracted to chocolate, the unavailable guy.

This is the core of what creates **level 2** people. Now the trigger is set for the daughter to be attracted to chocolate, boys and men who are emotionally unavailable / unattainable. These are males who will treat her just as her father did or worse. She will chase love that is unavailable, just as she competed with her father's world. She will compete for her man's attention against his work, hobbies, friends, or even his own children. If she were to get involved with a man that is a **level 1**, she will sabotage the relationship based on her conflicting ideas of what love is and the fact that the relationship will lack the excitement – the chase – that she gets from **level 2** men. By her mid-thirties, the salad becomes most attractive to her because the pain of her **level 2** relationships is too painful and she worries about her future. She then adapts to her Bob or she remains single, continuing on the treadmill of **level 2** relationships. Convinced she can change chocolate or that she is not going to concede for what she believes is less.

To a **level 2** person, readily available love is like a foreign language to their ears. It doesn't make sense and it doesn't hit the trigger. Had her father come home and was emotionally available and given her undivided attention, she would be more naturally attracted to men that are emotionally available. Ideally, Dad should come home from work and sit with his daughter for at least an hour. He should listen and give her sound and honest advice on life, love, men, and sex and uninterrupted attention.

The Robertson family is considered healthy and normal compared to most families. Imagine the conditioning children, especially girls, get in a family with more children. Imagine a household with two sisters and one brother all competing for Dad's attention after his long day at work. Imagine if the father doesn't come home until after everyone is asleep or he's not there at all. These circumstances have a tremendous negative effect on women. Dads need to come home and spend quality time with their daughters every day. The worst thing a dad can do is to ignore a daughter's emotional needs and concerns.

The parents don't understand that they are planting **level 2** triggers and wonder why their daughter is attracted to the wannabe musician. After years of this type of conditioning, children learn to seek attention elsewhere. Daughters who want dad's approval eventually realize that it's a losing battle, so they seek that need in other undesirable males (males that dad probably wouldn't approve of). They'll seek out males that are just as unavailable as their father has been. Without some guidance or self-esteem building, daughters could end up in the worst case scenario – working in an illicit business flaunting their bodies for men's validation and acceptance.

Like the Robertson's, most of us experience love and the triggers of love as something we have to compete for. Physically or spiritually, we want to receive and give love unconditionally. However from the time we are born, we are conditioned to do the contrary. I frequently pose the question to adults, "Do your parents know your favorite color?" The answer is usually no. Most parents don't know much about their children's inner feelings. Are parents too busy, are they fearful, or are they themselves just emotional incapable of such intimacy?

The father and daughter relationship is an interesting dynamic. Because men are not the best listeners and little girls love to talk, fathers unintentionally shut out their daughters. He tunes her out without knowing it, which results in her growing up needing an excessive amount of validation from a man. That is why women wear sexy clothes and ask questions that are self-validating, such as "Do I look good in this dress?" "Am I too fat?" "Do you really like me?"… Or the question that women ask after sex, "What does this mean?" This is also why marriage and wedding rings are so important to women. Marriage and a wedding ring is the ultimate validation by a man. Although these positive reinforcements help a woman's self-esteem, they are only a bandage for the bigger issue. The temporary fix leads her to constantly yearning for more.

The mother-son relationship is just as dramatic and also leads a boy to grow up to be a **level 2** man. The upside is that mothers usually don't bail out on the family. She is in the trenches through the thick and thin of it, even after the father may have made his exit. She is still interacting with her children by cooking, bandaging their wounds, cleaning, doing laundry, or helping with homework. Yet, the son is also taught that love is something you fight for. He too grows up engaging in relationships in which he competes for his woman's attention and validation.

Another influence that portrays the wrong message of love between **level 1** and **level 2 is** television and film, **level 1** entertainment. They sell what we all want, which is being in a **level 1** relationship, and it works. These media-driven ideas also lead us to believe we are waiting for our soul mate to arrive, like it happens in the movies, love songs, and romance novels. Other images tell us that if love is meant to be, it will be. These are all ideas created to entertain us.

Who would want to watch a movie featuring a boring **level 3** couple? Or…When the main characters' relationship starts off as a **level 1** and ends up as a **level 1** person? **Level 3** and **level 1** movies would be boring, lack character development, and character arc. The premise that sells entertainment are characters who start as **level 2** persons and ascend to **level 1** through consequences and circumstances. This is what we all seek and is the relationship Mimi wanted.

Chocolate Chip ~

Giving chocolate to others is an intimate form of communication, a sharing of deep, dark secrets. Milton Zelman, publisher of "Chocolate News"

Filling the Gap

The magnetic attraction that held Mimi and Jake together is that they filled each other's gap. When you meet your chocolate and your feel that you have an amazing chemistry with him, he serves as the vehicle for you to fill your gap and vice versus.

The day you are born your self-esteem is perfect; no issues, no concerns, no prejudices - no nothing. You are a perfect block of cheese. As you grow up you are being conditioned intentionally and unintentionally with positive and negative triggers by your parents, school, church, social circle, etc. The negative conditioning slowly chips away at your cheese - your self-esteem. Intentionally or unintentionally, your mother screams at you to stop crying when you are two months old. Your home economics teacher mutters that you are a slut underneath her breathe because you're dressed really cute one day and she looks like an old slob. Your English teacher says you'll never amount to much. Several female classmates snicker as you walk past them in the hallway and you think your jeans make you look fat. Your dad won't take the extra five minutes to listen to your side of the story. He yells and points a finger at you reinforcing that you are wrong. Somewhere in your psyche you think you aren't worthy of being listened to and your point of view is invalid. Unintentionally, each negative experience chisels away at your self-worth. For the record, those who chisel away at you are also challenged by their own low self-esteem issues. Their cheese too is no longer solid.

By the time you are eighteen years old, all of those self-esteem killer experiences have chopped your once perfect, solid block of cheese into Swiss. Cheese with holes equals self-esteem issues. You are not alone; your neighbors, cousins, friends, foes, the preachers, the teachers, and even the President of the United States are Swiss cheese. The world is populated with Swiss.

Another obvious example of self-esteem issues is seen with guests on the *Dr. Phil, Maury Povich,* and *Jerry Springer* shows. We think of *Dr. Phil's* guests as sophisticated people with mild self-esteem issues and *Springer's* guests as super dysfunctional people. Both guests have the same self-esteem issues. The difference between *Dr. Phil* and *Jerry Springer's* guests is how their self-esteem / Swiss cheese conditioning is expressed and acted out. *Dr. Phil's* guests are likely to be educated and not likely to physically fight. *Jerry Springer's* guests tend to be less educated and, as seen on television, will fight, scream, and shout to express their hurt feelings. Both shows' guests are casualties of Swiss cheese conditioning. Their solid block of cheese has been carved away over the years by criticism and poor examples. Both shows' guests love their chocolate. Without the Swiss cheese neither show would probably exist. The same goes for *The Maury Povich Show, The Montel Williams Show, TMZ, Entertainment Tonight,* and even the nightly news. The difference between the shows' guests is how they deal with their own Swiss cheese. *Dr. Phil* seeks an intellectual and positive solution, while *Springer's* guests seek a physical, angry, and volatile resolution. Everyone is included between these two extremes. Unfortunately, we are all the product of our environment. You are not alone.

You may have never realized that your once perfect cheese is now Swiss. What you see growing up is what you believe to be the truth. Growing up in your household where people communicated by screaming and putting each other down, you learned that's the way a family communicates. You grow up in one household so you never have another family to compare against yours. Besides, you trust your parents to give you the best tools to succeed in life. You take these truths, the good and the bad, with you into your adult life and adult relationships.

You leave the nest and you meet someone that you are crazy about, and you can't get enough and it feels so amazing. You feel the need to love this person with all of your soul and you say to yourself this is the one, this is my soul mate. Unbeknownst to you, your so called soul mate is a stranger who has their own Swiss cheese issues, but you never think about it or question it. All you know is that the relationship makes you feel good inside, a feeling you never felt before.

This stranger that you've met is the vehicle to temporary filling the holes in your Swiss cheese. Remember – the love you give him is the love you need, not the love he needs even though it seems that way. The love he gives you is the love he needs. It is like loving yourself vicariously through another person. You give him the things you want and how you want them. He does the same. It's deceiving because you think he is an amazing man who has magically tapped into your every emotional need. The magic, or the irony, is that you both are coincidentally the perfect vehicle to give yourselves exactly what you need to fill your cheese. Thus, you say I found my soul mate. I found "The One". The more you give, the better you feel as the gaps of your Swiss cheese are temporarily being filled with an impersonation of your once pure 100% perfect self-esteem solid block of cheese.

The major attraction to chocolate is that they make you feel needed physically and emotionally. This is what attracted Mimi to Jake. She felt he needed her. Her wanting to be needed is the biggest hole that needs to be filled, which is the same gap that is missing in her father / daughter relationship. Her dad never made her feel needed. Being needed is one of the stronger self-esteem boosters and it also fills another need – to feel significant. If you can tap into that experience, that feeling, you'll feel on top of the world.

Needing to fill the gaps becomes addictive. Addicts and / or addictions need their fix. Consider what happens after the first thirty to forty-five days in your relationship, when he begins to pull away? You freak out and tug on his sleeve to hold your dissolving relationship together. Or you say, "How can you do this to me?" "We have a connection and you said you love me, you said I was the one." You feel as though your world has fallen apart. You crave for him to come back or beg for him to stay and reconsider. You take him back pretty much under any circumstances; you just want him back.

As the holes of either one of you are filled up, one of you will eventually pull away, leaving your partner hanging. The first one to leave is the one who can have their Swiss cheese holes temporarily filled the fastest. In the beginning of the relationship you can't get enough of each other. It's actually a race with yourself to have your cheese/addiction fix. It becomes a race to see who can fill the holes first. It is not that you are intentionally competing with each other. You're addicted to the feeling and you want more and more. Once either partner's holes are filled up, they feel satisfied, content and confident, even though these feelings are only temporary. Everyone's tolerance to filling their needs varies. It took Jake less time to fill his gaps than Mimi.

Because of Jake's temporary confidence and blinded vision, he now sees Mimi as pathetic, needy, and weak. The more she yearns for Jake, the weaker she seems. Early in the relationship, she is the apple of his eye. Now he thinks, "What do we have in common besides lust? You are so needy – stop being weak and get your shit together because I got my shit together." Mimi bought into his belief, because he did seem confident and she seemed pathetic and needy, but she isn't weak at all. Why the imbalance? Because she is still chasing to him have all of her emotional gaps filled.

Whenever you want something that another person has you are in a submissive position, which can make you vulnerable and appear weak. Then, you don't rock the boat out of fear of losing them and the opportunity. Since Jake beat Mimi to the finish line and got his Swiss cheese to resemble his once solid block of cheese, she still needs to get her fix. She looks at Jake as though he has got it all together. Had the roles been reversed and Mimi gotten her gap filled first, she would look at him as weak, pathetic, and needy – the same way she sees Bob.

I am sure you've been with a guy that in the early stages of your relationship he was a challenge for you. You did everything to win him over and I mean any and everything he requested. Then one day he confesses his undying love for you. The next day you are bored. The more he admits his deep feelings, the more pathetic, weak and needy he seems to you. The more you pull away the more he feared his needs wouldn't be met. In that case your cheese is filled faster and you lost interest over night.

In Jake's temporary state of confidence he makes excuses to explain why the relationship is not working. He complains that you want to kiss and cuddle too much. That you want to hang out every day and you ask too many questions. Being in a submissive position, Mimi asked the fatal question, "What does it mean?"

There are endless excuses why things are not working out between Mimi and Jake. Mimi constantly feels she isn't good enough. She can't seem to ever make him happy. She wants things back to the days they first started dating. What does Mimi do? She works even harder to please him only to get the same results. Unbeknownst to Mimi, if Jake were truly a solid block of cheese (**level 1**) as he believes he is – confident and had his life together – he would have never been attracted to Mimi in the first place. Mimi can't see the truth. A pure **level 1** isn't attracted to a **level 2**; **level 2** is too unstable for a **level 1**.

People with rotating partners / serial daters are addicted to the high of having their emotional holes temporary refilled over and over again. It's a fantastic feeling. Imagine how you would feel every day if your cheese was as perfect as the day you were born. You would feel invincible. This is the feeling the addictive dater seeks. (There is nothing wrong with wanting that feeling).

Remember a time when you first fell in love or just started dating a guy, "The One", and you couldn't get enough of each other. Didn't you feel on top of the world? You look in the mirror and you like who you see. You go to work and love your job. You say hello and smile to your co-worker, whom just a week earlier you called a bitch underneath your breath. Your road rage is replaced with courteous gestures to other drivers. You might even leave a bigger tip than usual because money and the material things in life just don't matter at that point in time. To have or to sustain that feeling, some people move from relationship to relationship.

Six months into the relationship both parties' **level 2** issues rise to the surface. Then the relationship is not quite as fun. You are happy, but the thrill ride is over. Your block of cheese is definitely back to being Swiss. The bitch in the next cubicle really annoys you with her morning hellos. The traffic is unbearable; you never knew there were so many cars in the city. For some, the work that is necessary to sustain a relationship is too much. Especially when the pay off isn't the addictive high you get from filling the gap – the honeymoon stage of a relationship. Some people become frightened and leave in fear of working through the normal issues in any relationship. Some people leave a relationship as soon as their holes are temporarily filled. They can't handle the mundane feeling of their partner seeing them for who they really are. For example, a woman is dating a wannabe film director. In the beginning of their love affair he can build his self-worth to be more important than what he really is. His girlfriend buys into it, but the longer they date the more exposed he becomes. She will eventually see that the wannabe director isn't going to Warner Bros. Studios as he led her to believe, but instead he heads to Starbucks every morning. This guy has to bail on the relationship before he is discovered.

It is possible that maybe they fear they won't be liked, maybe they don't feel good enough, or fear they won't be able to live up to the relationship expectations. These types of concerns run through their minds. Leaving is the easy way out for them and the quick fix is to move on to another person and start all over again. Their new lover refills their holes temporarily and they both are in awe and amazement of each other – of course until they too have to confront the truth about their relationship once either person's holes are filled. Sometimes couples work through the filling of the cheese. Some stay in the relationship and find ways to fill their holes by having an affair. Both ways, the addiction will have its fix and one of you will get yours filled first.

If you have been in a situation where you've been dumped, you think he is an asshole. You gave your heart and soul to him and what did he do? He trampled all over it. Now you've taught yourself to believe that men and relationships suck. You say, "I'll never give my heart to another man." Understand that he does not know any better. He hasn't a clue about Swiss cheese. He is only reacting versus being pro-active emotionally. His confidence is only temporary. Besides it is not about him being loved, it's about you loving yourself.

The logic flaw in the Swiss Cheese Syndrome addiction is that the fix is temporary and the addiction can only be satisfied by the very person that has the same addiction, that person being chocolate, your Jake. Bob will never trigger that nerve inside you. If you want to feel whole, you date chocolate over and over again. You would think that the cure for your addiction would be the kind words and thoughtful gestures of salad. No, only a **level 2** dynamic – only they can be the vehicle to give you that amazing high of connection and love that is missing within. This is why even though a woman might eventually change her need and concede to be with a salad (Mr. Nice Guy), she will still crave her chocolate addiction.

As your temporary holes begin to decay, you feel the emptiness inside all over again. You look in the mirror and you don't like who you see. With all of the craziness and with all their insecurities and drama, chocolate does makes you feel whole. Chocolate will always be the one that got away and your first choice. With your cheese now being Swiss, you start the process over again in search of your new soul mate. You subconsciously seek relationships to fill the holes to become that solid block of cheese that you were told you were not. A relationship is simply two selfish strangers vying to be loved and having their needs met as quickly as possible and simultaneously.

Seeking the Addiction

The laws of attraction are deceiving. We've all heard the stories of couples meeting by chance, through online dating or on a blind date. We don't necessarily need to exchange words to know whether a person is emotionally available and wants nothing more than sex. The laws of attraction are always working to fill in the gaps. When you pass a stranger on the street that you find attractive or interesting, the laws of attraction are evaluating whether this person can fill in the gaps.

We pick up on a person's energy and selfishly know where they fit into our lives. When you see a guy with tattooed arms and driving a Harley, the energy doesn't scream, "Father of your kids." Visually that guy provokes the image of a bad boy, good times, parties, and great sex – not soccer coach. A guy that walks with a certain swagger you may read as being incredibly sexy, confident, and you thinking "Player," not "Priest." When Mimi met Jake, it is Jake's persona of being a soul she could help and that makes him attractive. She knows he is a challenge and subconsciously she seeks him out to have her Swiss cheese filled. The laughter, the songs, the sex that Jake gives her are token gifts. Jake needing Mimi is the real icing on the cake. The bottom line is that she can only give him what she is missing. She makes that subconscious decision in the first ten minutes of meeting Jake. If she would have perceived him as too available and nice, their relationship would have lasted only eleven minutes.

In the relationships that seem too good to be true and that are magical, the magic is your gaps, your holes being filled. Both people are going to race to have the holes filled as soon as possible. It's addictive and it feels amazing. You've heard a friend of yours tell you that they met an amazing guy. That's him. You ever wonder what happen to Mr. Amazing and why they are no longer together. Now she is on to her new Mr. Amazing.

The addictive relationship can last for one night or one decade. It depends on how quickly or slowly they can fill their gaps. Most relationships are based on the refilling of the gaps. When the gaps are back, they are refilled through events in the couple's lives. The lust is gone until your man is promoted and is getting more recognition. Now you find yourself competing for his attention, your trigger is released again and you can't get enough. Whether or not a couple stays together or your man leaves, you don't have to complain to your friends about his behavior. You don't have to talk about how much he changed from the day you met him. From the very beginning of the relationship, see him for who he really is. Don't let your heart get carried away and lose sight of what is real. Keeping yourself grounded and clear can have him chasing you indefinitely because he needs his gaps filled. Stop beating yourself up and feeling like you'll never live up to his expectations or that you are pathetic, needy, or weak. The truth is he got to the finish line before you did. That's it and that's all there is.

Unfortunately, the addiction is so strong that we sometimes do irrational things, like get married to a man we've only known for a month. Women also foolishly have a baby with a man who is married. Even more common when you get caught in the whirlwind of having your gaps filled, you are the first to open your hand and lend him money. You buy him gifts or co-sign on a car loan for him. Then after the thrill is gone, you are stuck with a child, a deadbeat dad, and paying for a car you never drive or in a miserable marriage with a man you barely know.

An example - Justin and Tracy's marriage ended on pretty bad terms. After the divorce, Tracy got involved with another man named Oscar. Tracy and Oscar got together as a result of Justin and Tracy constantly bickering over the years, because Oscar is the shoulder for Tracy to cry on. He portrayed himself as her knight in shining armor. Over the years Tracy trusted Oscar and everyone saw them as great friends. Oscar is that guy who cowardly waits in the wings for your relationship to fall apart. He is too spineless to seek out his own relationship. He becomes your understanding and compassionate understudy / best friend.

Once Justin and Tracy were separated, Oscar conveniently started dating Tracy. Whenever Tracy complained to Oscar about her ex-husband, Oscar who hardly knew Justin would side with Tracy and together point their fingers and with expletives go on about how much of a jerk Justin is. Instead of maybe showing Tracy ways to reconcile what is left of Justin and Tracy's relationship or encourage her not to be nasty during the divorce, Oscar encouraged her malicious behavior. Their comradery gave them connection, especially for Oscar. He is desperate to be loved and have the attention Tracy gave him. She eventually became his addiction. In this case, they both got their holes filled at the same time at the expense of her ex-husband, Justin. After six months, Tracy and Oscar's hot and heavy relationship cooled off. Better yet, Tracy, being the more secure of the two, filled her holes up the fastest. Tracy and her ex began speaking on civil terms with each other, which also accelerated her holes being filled.

Oscar is the perfect guy to help fill her gap. She wanted to feel love, connection, and appreciation at a time that she was being rejected by her ex-husband, Justin. As Tracy got back into a normal routine within her new lifestyle she needed Oscar less and less. Indeed, he began to bore her. The less she needed him, the more he held on. His panic button kicked in and he needed his fix. When emotionally holding on to Tracy backfired, he would call and harass the ex-husband. He is hoping that by starting a fight with him, Tracy would be on the same page and bad mouth Justin. Then he and Tracy would have the same connection like in the past. Unfortunately for Oscar, the ex-husband shook off his harassing phone calls and Tracy saw his behavior as childish. Little did Oscar realize that his first thirty days had passed! Tracy felt fulfilled and didn't need him anymore. Being the weaker of the two, his gap is left half filled. Needless to say, Tracy and Oscar did not last much longer after that.

FYI – No other person can fix or cure your low self-esteem (Swiss cheese) or give you permanent high self-esteem. Although chocolate can supply some temporary relief, only you can build up your own self-worth. If you invest in the necessary time to do the necessary self-help work, then one day you will look in the mirror and like what you see. Only you can permanently make your cheese whole.

White Chocolate ~

"Good Living is an act of intelligence, by which we choose things which have an agreeable taste rather than those which do not." Brillat-Savarin

Setting Terms & Conditions

In every aspect of your life you enter into a written agreement. E.g. your lease agreement for your apartment, your purchase agreement with the auto dealership, the credit card agreement with your bank, your contract for employment, and your agreement with your household utilities. Before you are asked to sign your signature on the dotted line of any contract stating that you understand the terms and conditions (marriage license being the exception), you are asked to read the contract. Every contract comes with terms and conditions clearly stating the amount due, the duration, the interest, and the consequences if you default on the terms, and so forth. Sometimes some institutions that grant you credit go as far as to give you terms and conditions verbally. Every contract says that if you are negligent, miss, or stop making payments, per the contract terms, there are consequences, such as sending your negative repayment history to all three credit report agencies, closing your account, foreclosure, or repossession of property.

It's a simple concept we all understand because we've all signed our name on the dotted line at one time or another. The $64,000 dollar question is why is it that when it comes to your relationship, whether it is casual or committed and especially in a marriage, the terms or conditions are not spelled out as they are with all other contracts? You probably have been in many relationships and you have signed your name on a contract, figuratively speaking.

We all use or have heard the expressions: "If you cheat on me, I'm leaving you," "Why didn't you call..." or we say something similar to that as form of contractual agreement. These inconsequential affirmations do not establish concrete boundaries; they really are not terms and conditions. They leave a lot of room for interpretation and misinterpretation. The reason we have contracts with terms and conditions is so that both parties involved avoid misrepresentation of what is agreed upon.

Consider what would happen if the auto dealership sold you a vehicle without a contract, but rather a handshake agreement. Think about the havoc you would have in your life if you were granted a credit card or bought a house without terms or conditions. You would live in fear, as you do in your relationship. You would fear that the credit card company would raise your interest rate whenever they felt it is in their best interest and basically renege on what you thought you had agreed upon in the handshake. You would stress out thinking the bank would at any time foreclose on your house or sell your house to another buyer while you were sleeping. Think about the parallel correlation to not having terms and conditions in your business life and your personal life. Your relationship would resemble Jake and Mimi's; just as the buyer wouldn't know how many late payments it would take before repossession and the seller wouldn't know when the payments were due. Sadly, these are the types of feelings people experience every day in their relationship. You can't sleep thinking about where your guy might be, whom he might be with, where, and why. The next time you see him is he going to tell you he found another woman and it's over? You might fear that when your cell phone rings it is another woman telling you your man got her pregnant. Can you feel the anxiety just reading this?

Marriage is one of the most sacred and important decisions in your life. Ironically, we ignore one of the most important factors in marriage's success: the terms and conditions. We are too much in love and ignore any impulse of warning signs that you may need some boundaries. Like Mimi, we are too afraid to demand or discuss, in written or verbal form, the detailed terms or conditions of your relationship for fear it will diminish the intensity. When you ask your partner for boundaries he retorts with, "You don't trust me?" Others are too embarrassed or fear confrontation and rejection.

The only terms and conditions that are discussed are written in your vows, e.g. "til death do us part"... "In sickness and health"...etc. Even, then those terms and conditions are not discussed in detail; and what does –"til death do us part" mean in terms of boundaries? Does it mean you agree on how you'll disagree or communicate? Where in your vows is it written that you will agree to disagree or discuss your differences or how to resolve your differences? With a 50% divorce rate "...'til death do us part" is beside the point.

The irony of the terms and conditions of marriage is that if the day should come and you divorce, your attorney and the courts will want in detail the terms and conditions of your dissolution of marriage. They will demand that both parties write their expense summary of assets and debts. If there are children involved, the court will be very specific regarding the day, time, and location for visitation and the amount you will receive or pay for child support. The same is true if there is alimony to be awarded. The court will request tax returns, payroll stubs, copies of your pension plan, property and bank statements. The court wants your personal finances in detail. All the details that a married couple avoided and thought unnecessary will become clear cut during the divorce proceedings. If you and your partner can't come to a reasonable win – win resolution, the attorneys, the judge, and the state laws will dictate how the property is divided and exactly how much you are going to pay or receive in alimony, and when, where, and how you see your kids.

Why not have terms and conditions outlined before the wedding day comes to pass. It might save your relationship. If divorce is your last option, I'm certain that the dissolution of your marriage will be low to no-drama as a result of having clear and definitive boundaries and terms in the first place. *If you did not communicate during pre-matrimony and during your married years; you certainly aren't going to communicate amiably during the divorce proceedings* (e.g. Jake and Mimi). As Dr. Phil says, "The person you marry isn't the person you divorce."

Terms and conditions that truly define a relationship are:

- How are you going to agree to disagree?
- How do we agree to share household responsibilities? How often are we going to have sex?
- Why or why shouldn't you share a banking account?

- What kind of debt do you have and how do you plan to resolve it?
- What are your financial goals?
- What does money mean to you?
- Who will be in charge of making the money?
- How are you going to be responsible for your own actions?
- If we break any of the above agreements what are the consequences?
- What will it take for us to end the relationship?
- If we end our relationship, let's agree on how we resolve our differences.

The questions that you ask and answers are unique to your relationship. However, every relationship, regardless of how new – casual booty or marriage – all need terms and conditions. Don't fool yourself. Actually friends with benefits do have good terms and conditions.

Another aspect of relationships that, if not outlined with terms and conditions from the very beginning, will cause relationship failure is sex. Couples need to agree as to how much sex they want or don't want and what are they willing to give. It is very difficult to discuss your sexual needs, wants, and desires days or weeks after you've been having sex. We are usually too embarrassed to ask for what we really want or we are fearful of hurting our partner's feelings. Once you start having sex one way and you partner is doing something you really don't like, and then you ask for what you really want, they think to themselves, "Why didn't she tell me how she wanted it in the beginning? What else are you dissatisfied about?" When you have a disagreement, and you will, establish how you will resolve your differences. Anticipating having differences is a good thing. Remember you are from one part of the world and he is from another.

For you hopeless romantics, yes there are couples who happen to be incredibly compatible, but not on every level. Even if they are amazingly compatible they will have disagreements. Furthermore, as far as we know, they might have verbalized the boundaries of their relationship; all we see is the result of their efforts.

For your own protection, don't get your hopes up so high that you think your dream relationship doesn't need terms and conditions. If you are lucky to meet the perfect match that requires no work, then fantastic. If it's that perfect and if it does call for terms, you'll be prepared.

Enter your relationship with the expectation that terms and conditions are and will be necessary. As much as Dr. Phil and his wife appear to be the model married couple, they are probably smart enough to continually negotiate and renegotiate the boundaries of their relationship. Don't be afraid or believe that something is wrong with you or the relationship because you need to discuss boundaries. The worst case scenario is that it will bring you both closer together. Chocolate needs boundaries and certainly terms.

Logically, it makes sense that we all enter into a verbal or written contract in our business lives. Yet when it comes to our relationships we enter them with reckless abandonment. I have to admit that without boundaries, there is definitely a high level of built-in excitement, spontaneous forbidden public sex or late night sex at 4:30am. Living in uncertainty is thrilling, e.g. the thrill Jake gives Mimi. Unfortunately, with the thrill comes pain, anxiety, and fear. The end result is destruction. Jake set his own terms and conditions. Mimi had hers, but she never reinforced them. He would see her when he wanted under the conditions that she supported. Mimi's feeble terms and conditions were that Jake spends reasonable time with her. Reasonable time as defined by Jake, not Mimi – leaving her abandoned. She accepted things as they were because when she did see him, she is ecstatic. If you seek the thrill and can handle the thrill and all you want is the thrill, more power to you. Go for it and enjoy yourself. Just don't expect your Jake to behave like Bob. A thrill ride is just that, a thrill.

Another factor is that we fear that setting terms somehow negates the fun of a relationship. You are afraid that the fun and spontaneity between the two of you will be lost, but in actuality the contrary is true. I blame society, the media industry, parenting, and marketing images of relationships for us having these utopian ideals of how relationships should work. We are taught that love between two people just happens, with a belief system that if it is true love or love at first sight the terms and conditions are automatically understood between two people. The irony is that these two people who fall in love at first sight are indeed strangers. They need terms and conditions as much as the next couple, maybe more. Let's face it, you are from Green Bay, Wisconsin, the youngest of three girls, you are catholic with strict parents, a controlling mother, and a passive father. He is from Los Angeles, California the elder of two step-brothers; raised by his mother and stepfather, and his family is non-religious. As much as you love each other, you both are from different worlds. It is the same as going into contract with your landlord whom you instantly got along with and you loved the apartment, a match made in heaven, if you have terms and conditions.

Honestly, would you engage in a business transaction with a stranger without a contact? Would you purchase a vehicle from a stranger under the assumption that there is chemistry between you both and therefore no contract is necessary? Would you rent an apartment to someone you just met, and not run a credit check or references? And do this all in the name of "If it is meant to be, it will be?" The answer is no absolutely not. The absurdity of it is that it's done every day in every relationship.

Don't be mistaken and believe that because you and your new love have so much in common that you don't need to discuss terms or conditions. In fact, throughout the life of your relationship you should consistently re-evaluate your terms and conditions with your partner and make new terms as you cross new thresholds. After five years in your relationship you have to decide as a couple to buy a refrigerator. Your Jake is a gadget man and wants the refrigerator with all the bells and whistles. You are looking for more freezer storage space and a design to blend in with the rest of the kitchen appliances. Before you make the purchase or even start looking at a refrigerator, agree on how you are going to disagree. The day might come when you decide to take a vacation. You like to mosey along and look at all the tourist sites. He loves to see as much as he can in a single day. This crossroad is another opportunity to agree on how you are going to disagree. Without some terms and conditions on traveling you'll be stuck on a miserable vacation.

Every parent immediately establishes terms and conditions for children, even a newborn. The mother stops running at the baby's beck and call when he crying in the middle of the night after three months or so. She does this to set the terms and conditions of the relationship between her and the child. Who hasn't grown up to understand that bad behavior equals some sort of punishment, based on the terms and conditions your parents instituted? We all understand the importance of terms and conditions from the point of view of parents, child, lessee, employee, citizen, customer, business owner, and a one-night-stand to name a few.

There are terms and conditions for a one-night stand or friend with benefits situation. In fact, the one-night-stand / booty call / friend with benefits, or whatever you call it, has terms and conditions that are more clearly defined than a marriage. Those terms are very clear: 1) We are not in a relationship 2) I don't want to get to know you better 3) I really don't care about you as a person other than to see that you satisfy my needs 4) Don't call me, and I won't call you unless you want to have sex 5) Thank you for the great time, until next time take care. Those terms are crystal clear. If you have ever been in a friend with benefits relationship, you hardly ever argue or have jealous feelings! The same is true for call girls – the men get what they pay for.

Setting the terms and conditions has to happen in the very beginning of the relationship. Get the conversation started within the first week. I'm not suggesting that you spring a ton of demands on you new potential partner, but you should set the terms on how often you are going talk on the phone during the week or how late you accept his phone calls. The terms and conditions only apply to the level of your relationship. Friends with benefits terms and conditions won't apply to the married couple and vice versus.

If you wait until you are knee deep in the relationship it's going to be too late. You have already established non – verbal terms and conditions. It will take some great people skills for Mimi to convince Jake to stay in bed and cuddle with her after sex. Why should he? Things are great the way they are, on his terms.

It's easy to be lazy and not want to set boundaries in the beginning of the relationship because it feels so good. Who wants to rock the boat of a good thing by talking about boundaries and terms and conditions? It's like taking a pair of high heels that you look so sexy in – the last thing you want to do is talk about the price.

You don't care about the terms and conditions until your relationship crashes and burns; he isn't returning your calls, he forgot your favorite holiday, and he only shows up in the middle of the night. At this point you'll gladly set some terms and conditions. In fact, you'll do your best to instill some order, but usually in the form of demands. Had you remained calm and looked at the bigger picture you wouldn't have been in your present soured relationship. Remember, although the shoes are hot and you look sexy wearing them to the party, you still have to pay for those expensive shoes.

Prenuptial Terms and Conditions

If you are planning to get married, do yourself a favor when you order the flowers arrangements, buy your wedding dress, and write your vows, get a prenuptial agreement. A prenuptial agreements states the terms and conditions you would otherwise be unaware of until the dreaded divorce. How many people do you think know the divorce laws of their state? My guess is not many. I am not an advocate of divorce, but I believe the more you have in writing between the two of you the better. Even if you're prenuptial said you agreed to split everything 50 / 50 from the day of your marriage forward, at least you know what the terms are. My belief is that the more you write out your needs and wishes, the clearer you both are to each other. Then the boundaries are clearly stated and your relationship runs smoothly.

Another trap to be aware of is how organized religion being comprised of God, the Bible, the church and its leaders, sometimes disrupts your better judgment. Case in point, Rabbi Steven Z. Leder, located in Los Angeles, authored a book entitled, *More Money than God: Living a Rich Life without Losing Your Soul*. He explores how money affects families, friends, ethics, and feelings of self-worth. Amongst his many topics, he discusses prenuptial agreements and how they cause grief between couples. I thought to myself, red flag – let me investigate a little further. He goes on to say that he believes that prenuptial agreements pre-suppose that marriage will end in divorce. He also said that you have to find a woman/man you can trust, which would eliminate the need for a prenuptial agreement. I spent a few days contemplating this idea. Then it hit me that a man of God is telling couples they don't need a prenuptial agreement, when in fact, in every aspect of our lives and in his we sign agreement documents. I'm not judging Rabbi Leder or his book as right or wrong. The point is the Rabbi signed an agreement when he handed his finished manuscript to his book publisher Bonus Books. It was an agreement that was scrutinized by his attorney as well as Bonus Books' attorneys. Why didn't he find a publisher that he really trusted and who really trusted him? That way all he would have to do is shake hands on the deal. Being an intelligent man, he knew it is in his best interest to know in writing exactly what the consequences were. He wanted to know what the terms and conditions were if the book sells a certain amount of copies. He wanted to know how many copies would be printed and how much money he would make on each copy sold. By signing a legal contract he doesn't pre-suppose that his book will succeed or fail.

I think that most Americans have good credit and are honest people. I can assure you that if the Rabbi owned a car dealership no matter how great your credit is, he would make you sign on the dotted line before you drove off in your brand new car. Signing on the dotted line doesn't pre-suppose that you will default on the loan. It is only an agreement of the terms and if you do default, the consequences are clearly stated. So the question is what is the difference between a publishing agreement and a prenuptial agreement? They both set the terms and conditions so that you can sleep at night. Besides, as you read this book, I am sure you would agree a prenuptial is necessary because your partner, regardless of what the Rabbi thinks, is a stranger you are getting to know better. No matter how well you think you know your partner, you don't.

God

When it comes to matters of the heart we sometimes throw caution to the wind. Whatever happens will happen, or my favorite, "If God wants us to be together, it will be." In a television interview, Janet Jackson is commenting on her two previous marriages and the possibility of a third to Jermaine Dupree. Basically, she said that marriage isn't for everyone and that she isn't sure if she would do it again unless it is in God's plan. I understand the point she is making, but was it God's plan that she have a wardrobe malfunction during her performance at the Super Bowl? Or better yet, was it God's plan that she invests her money wisely? Was it God's plan to make her a superstar or is it hard work and great advisers? By the way, I'm a huge fan of Janet Jackson. Sometimes in love we hide behind God and then make God responsible for the success or failure of our relationships. You certainly didn't graduate from college with that attitude - you studied. You don't rely on God to pay your bills. You go to work forty hours each week.

Overall, I do think that organized religion, God, Church, and the Bible serve a greater good for mankind. However, be aware of how your religious values affect you in your relationships. These triggers are, for the most part, made with the best of intentions, but the results can be negative and ultimately hinder our ability to fulfill our sexual, emotional, and ironically, your spiritual desires. I want to emphasize that I'm not making a mockery of God, religion, or criticize your beliefs. I'm saying, instead of saying; "If it's God's will," take control of your relationship and life. Maybe everything we do is predetermined and happens whether or not God wants it to. I would imagine that somewhere in the Universe in God's master plan he won't be mad at you for seeking knowledge about relationships and setting clear terms and conditions.

Preparing the Terms and Conditions

In preparing the terms and conditions, you are going to determine what type of terms and conditions you need in the first seven days of dating. On each date ask probing questions that will help you determine what terms and conditions you need for your new relationship. Ask how do you feel about monogamy? How do you resolve your differences? What really makes you jealous? Spend less conversation on the usual stuff such as, where are you from? Or... Where were you raised? Do a lot of listening while you are mesmerized by your Jake. If you listen over the next seven days, you'll learn most of what you need to know about him, well at least enough to make a decision to move the relationship forward or not. Most people can't hide their true self for very long. On the first date everyone has their guard up, but by the seventh date they are more comfortable. The more comfortable they are, the more their true self will be revealed. We are so in awe of our new found love that we only want to hear what we want to hear.

When you're beautiful and sexy, Jake said, I don't believe in working 9am to 5pm. It is a red flag, but you chose to ignore the sign. You rather hear the story about the time he saved his sister from drowning or the time he fought off a ten-foot Boa Constrictor. Then you think to yourself – my hero, he's cute, he's chivalrous, and dangerous, just the way I like my chocolate. In the course of the conversation between the heroic tales, ask questions regarding your and his comfort zone and boundaries. In the end you'll have the terms and conditions that your relationship will ultimately need.

Assorted Chocolate ~

"This guy found a bottle in the ocean, and he opened it and out popped a genie, and he gave him three wishes. The guy wished for a million dollars, and poof! There was a million dollars. Then he wished for a convertible, and poof! There was a convertible. And then, he wished he could be irresistible to all women... poof! He turned into a box of chocolates." Anonymous

Our Fundamental Needs

In order for Jake and Mimi to be the best for each other, it is important that they understand the essential humans needs. In a relationship and in your personal life you need to know what your needs are and if they are being met. The problems in relationships are due to our needs not being met by our partner. They are not being met either because they don't always know exactly what their needs are, as in the case of Jake and Mimi, or unfortunately they don't care to meet them.

What are our needs? Needs are what drive us to wake up in the morning, to seek love, to eat, to work, to succeed, and unfortunately for some, they have a need to fail. Man has a need to protect and provide; therefore, he will not miss work and see to it that his family is fed. A woman has a need to nurture. She will of course see to it that her children are loved. Some people have the need to be the best. Our needs assist us in working towards a purpose or against a purpose.

Our needs are so strong we will work hard to meet them regardless of how they affect others. Let's say your Jake, who is usually a homebody, starts working at Gold's Gym to gain muscle mass or buys a red sports car and receives a lot of attention from the opposite sex. As a result, he flirts more blatantly with females at the gym. His new behavior is unacceptable to you, so you react by getting angry and a fight ensues. You tell him that you are not comfortable or are hurt by the way he now ignores you and gives other women attention. You explain to him that his behavior could lead to other things such as infidelity and the end of your relationship. He sees that he is hurting you, but he doesn't stop his behavior because his need to feel significant, which his muscles and attention gives him, is greater than his need to please you. Personal needs and wants will always win over the needs for others. Unless your own need is to help others.

We will even abandon our moral beliefs, our religious upbringing, and family values to meet that need. In the huge pornography industry, I'm certain most males and females that perform explicit sexual acts are in conflict with the moral beliefs and values they learned at home. As immoral as these acts may seem, why do people continue to do them? Again, because their need for connection, uncertainty, and significance is so strong that they choose the attention they receive over what they believe is right or wrong. I'm not judging the pornography business. This is just an example of how strong and important our needs are and the lengths we will go to have them met. Be aware of your needs and your partner's needs; this will dictate their behavior one way or another.

Significance

There are many ways we can have this need met. One of the quickest ways for a woman to feel significant is to dress sexy for the attention of men. The minute a guy whistles at her she feels important, as it validates her significance. A good kid might join a street gang to feel connected or even murder someone to feel more important that his victim. Another way to instantly feel significant is to put others down, although you know it is wrong and it doesn't feel good. If you are in a relationship and your partner is belittling you, it is one of their ways of feeling significant. When they are struggling through their day or careers, when things don't seems to be going their way, you might find them being more critical of you. We are going to find our significance one way or another.

There are people who work at the same job for the same low pay for years. They'll even put in overtime and never bill the company. These people could be more talented than their present occupation, but instead of wanting to be promoted they remain there for years. The reason for this is that their job or title gives them the significance and importance that they all need. To be promoted or receive a raise might not meet his needs. There is a guy who is a handyman for a company I used to work for named Jim. I asked Jim, who had been with the company for twenty years, "Don't you want to be promoted to a better position than being the in-house handyman?" He said "No," and then he pulled out a key ring that must have had 100 keys on it. Then he said, "You see these keys," I said "Yeah." He said, "I have a key to every lock in this building…these keys make me feel more important than any executive position."

In your personal life and your career, you should know what your needs are and when they are or are not being met. There are negative and positive ways to have your needs met. If you know what your needs are, you can make positive adjustments when you are seeking to have your needs met and not make negative choices.

These Are the Six Basic Needs for All Humans:

1. THE NEED FOR CERTAINTY — Knowing you have a job, that there is food in the refrigerator, or that you are loved.

2. THE NEED FOR UNCERTAINTY — Having spontaneous sex, sex with a new partner, following a young celebrity, irrational behavior, or watching a movie and not knowing the outcome.

3. THE NEED FOR SIGNIFICANCE — Validation for your efforts or knowing that you are important to your parents, significant other, or most importantly to yourself.

4. THE NEED FOR CONNECTION — Having a family gives you a feeling of connection, being on a team, or part of a group.

5. THE NEED TO CONTRIBUTE — Giving of your abundance: money, love, or knowledge to help others.

6. THE NEED FOR GROWTH — To be better, lose weight, be a better partner, grow spiritually, and learn more.

Another fundamental need is the need in which you feel **_most_** loved. Below is a list of ways in which we all can feel loved. The question is which one makes you feel the **_most_** loved?

Which Way Do You Feel Most Loved?

BEING HELD — Being held by your partner

TO BE LOOKED IN THE EYES — Your partner making eye-to-eye contact

TO BE SHOWN — Your partner giving to you or doing something for you

TO BE TOLD — Your partner expressing their words of affection to you

At the beginning of their relationship, Mimi should have asked Jake which way he felt most loved; being held, looked in the eyes, being shown, or being told. The way in which he feels loved is based on the trigger that is planted between him and his first experience of love – mother, grandmother, or aunt. As a kid, my trigger is planted to be shown love. Now as an adult I feel most loved when being shown to me by a woman. Being told, being looked in the eyes, and being held are great, but if you show me, you've got me.

A college friend of mind named Christopher became a successful Attorney and CPA. After achieving success in his career and dating many incompatible women, Christopher finally fell in love with the beautiful and sexy Tara. A year later they had a beautiful wedding in Santa Barbara, CA. In his moment of bliss, Christopher bought Tara a new Range Rover for her birthday. To show his love and appreciation Christopher had a house built for Tara on the beach in Laguna Hills, CA. It took a year and a half to complete construction and furnish what turned out to be an amazing house.

About a week or so after moving in, they took a Saturday night to relax and spend some quality time together. Christopher and Tara built a romantic fire and sipped wine. Tara looked Christopher in the eyes and asked him if he loved her. After years of hard work Christopher is proud of his accomplishments, his career, his relationship, and building his dream home. Christopher stood up and walked to the bay window that overlooked the Pacific Ocean, crossed his arms, looking at Tara he paused for a minute and said, "Look around you." A week later, Tara filed for divorce. What Christopher didn't know is that Tara felt most loved being told, not shown. She wanted him to tell her how much he loved her. Christopher felt most loved by being shown. Therefore, he showed her how much he loved her. With all the gifts she is given by Christopher she never felt love. As the story ends Christopher is left numb and never understanding why she left.

Most of us give love to our partner based on how we experience and define what love is. This is a common conflict in a relationship. All you have to do is ask your partner which way they feel most loved, then love them that way. If they feel most loved being told, tell them. Sometimes we want to change how a person should feel most loved, remember we like what we like. They want to be told but you are showing them. Then you complain that they don't appreciate your hard work.

Controlling Your States

Lastly, in your relationship and personal life you have to know what state of mind you are in at all times. You have to know why you are happy and unhappy or why you are succeeding or failing. When you are unaware of your state of mind, we tend to point fingers at others when things are not going well. We believe that it is them, not us, which is causing our happiness or unhappiness. Note this common phrase, "You made me mad." No one makes you mad. You chose to pick that state of mind as a response to those words or actions. In order to know what state of mind you are in you have to be willing to be completely honest with yourself. No one is responsible for your self-esteem issues.

Instead of pointing fingers, learn why you are not happy or why you feel unsettled inside. Study yourself when you are experiencing happiness or sadness. You can get yourself out of the state of sadness and into the state of happiness by doing the things that make you happy. You need to know what it is that makes you happy. If you are feeling depressed, stop and ask yourself if it is the room you're in, the clothes you're wearing, the weather, the choice you've made, etc. When you are in a state of bliss, ask the same types of questions. Stop being reactive and be pro-active. In the book *7 Habits of Highly Successful People* the author Stephen Convey talks about the circle of concern versus the circle of influence. In the circle of concern, to put it simply, are things you can't control - the weather, other people, traffic, and so on. The circle of influence you can control because you are the circle of influence. Get to know yourself better, be pro-active, and choose which state you want to be in. Before you make a judgment call, be sure to look in the mirror first and see that it's not you.

The Myths of Relationships

1. Infatuation equals love. It never has and never will equal love. Infatuation is just that – infatuation.

2. If it isn't perfect, it isn't meant to be. Relationships take work. No one is perfect, and neither is a relationship.

3. Once love dies, you can never get it back. Of course you can. Ex-lovers, ex-husbands, and ex-wives get back together all the time. Like anything in life you can make a mistake and couples do realize that they prefer to stay together than to be separated.

4. Chemistry is all that matters. Chemistry is very important, but it is not everything. Other things are just as important, such as communication and sexuality.

5. There is one true soul mate for everyone. I don't believe in soul mates. There are many people that you can love and be in love with. If you live long enough, you'll experience love more than once.

6. Love conquers all. I never understood this one. Conquer all of what?

7. *You can't rekindle passion. Like number 3, given the right circumstances, couples and even ex-couples can have passion. A couple could be stressed due to finances. Once they resolve their financial issues the stress goes away and passion is rekindled.*

8. *If you are really in love you won't be attracted to other people. Having an attraction for a person other than your mate is natural and doesn't mean you are not committed to the relationship or in love. Being attracted to someone else doesn't mean you should act on that attraction. If you are attracted to tall, dark, and handsome men, you will probably see them when you are out and about, so why not look and appreciate the view.*

9. *If you meet the right person, you will live happily ever after. This is true if you put the necessary work into the relationship. Just because he is the right person doesn't mean it will automatically be happiness forever after.*

10. *If a relationship is tough, it means you have the wrong partner. All relationships are tough. When things get tough in your relationship, and they will, you have to work through them.*

11. *In marriage, you become one. You don't. You are from Wisconsin and your guy is from Los Angeles.*

12. *When you get married, you will get unlimited sex. Wrong. Ultimately, you'll get less than if you were single. Resentment gets in the way of passion. Also, both parties can become content and lazy.*

13. *Your husband or guy will respect you because you are married or in a committed relationship. Wrong. Respect is*

consistently earned throughout the life of the relationship from one partner to another. If you are unemployed and the wife becomes the breadwinner, she will lose some respect for. Don't fool yourself.

14. You can lower your guard and be a couch potato. Not true, you have to stay aware of your relationship and where you are in the relationship. Know when it's time to step up your game. As we grow older, our needs change. Stay on top of your relationship and adjust to those changes.

15. You're lucky to get sex. It's not luck if you are in an adult relationship. It's an act that adults do and want. It's each of your responsibility to see to it that your partner's sexual needs are met. Otherwise, what is the point of being in a relationship? Luck is in Las Vegas when you inadvertently wind up in bed with your dream movie star (Brad Pitt) because there is only one hotel room in town. And in the room there is only one twin size bed left and they have to share a room with you for the whole weekend. That's some luck.

In all relationships there is a constant need to grow and evolve. Some evolve slower or faster than others. Realize that you are two individuals in a partnership with common goals for the success of the relationship. Although we are strangers to each other, it doesn't mean we can't have the love we desire. Just be aware that you are from different backgrounds with different rules of engagement. Also, you must not sit on your laurels. Just because he is your significant other doesn't mean you can become lazy in your relationship. Use the truism that we really don't know each other to communicate and learn who your partner is. Your relationship doesn't have to be like your parent's relationship, or like a television show, e.g. My Wife and Kids, I Love Lucy, or The Cosby Show, and certainly not like Jake and Mimi's.

Over 30 – Intelligence

Another important myth for women managing their chocolate is how men feel about intelligence. This point is very important for women to understand, especially those in their thirties or older. A thirty-something or older woman is seasoned in her career – self reliant and independent. She probably has her own home, has good credit, and can afford the things in life she requires. She doesn't necessarily need a man to take care of her. A common complaint I hear from women in this group is that men are intimidated by their intelligence and professional careers. Generally speaking this is not true.

These women are taught that they had to be intelligent, self-reliant, and independent. Self-reliance and independence is great for both sexes. The confusion is that women were also taught that intelligent, self-reliant, and independent women are a man's need. They are wants not needs for men; therefore, men are not intimated by intelligence. If a man doesn't find a professional woman attractive, it's probably because he is just not attracted to her.

A thirty-year-old professional woman would potentially date a man five years younger to twenty years older. And if he is not a Jake then he is probably a working professional himself; versus a man forty-plus-year-old whose dating options are eighteen to forty-five years old plus. You have to understand and accept what men are looking for. First of all it is physical. Men want attractive women. Secondly, men want to be taken care of. A turn off for some men is the fact that you are a professional and are not available to take care of him, both of which he can find in a twenty-something year old. The twenty-something is just starting her career and has fewer responsibilities in her life; therefore, is readily available. And the fact that she is twenty and beautiful is also an incentive. It is not the women's intelligence that turns him off. I'm not saying there are no exceptions and that one is better than the other. However, attraction is a preference.

Short term, the working professional is great – long term, it's going to be an issue. Men don't want their women gone all day and working late nights. I'm generalizing – Yes, there are some men who prefer professional working women, but generally speaking men prefer a woman who is going to be home when he gets home. I understand the economics of supporting a household and that two people sometimes need to work to make ends meet. That aside, at the fundamental level, men want a woman that is available at home.

Honestly, I've never heard any of my male friends directly or indirectly tell me they were intimidated by a woman's intelligence. What's more, I don't think men look for intelligence the way women imagine. Men want smart and intelligent women. They want to be able to carry on an intelligent conversation, but I've never heard a guy say how turned on he is by a woman's high I.Q. Playboy doesn't sell intelligence; it sells sexuality to men, as does television and films. They profit quite well. The media is most honest about what turns men on – sex! They don't sell intelligence, they sell sex, and sex sells. If men's need is for intelligence, you'd better believe the entertainment business would be all over it. I'm not saying men don't like smart women. What I am saying is that rarely are men turned off or intimidated by a woman's intelligence. An uneducated man is probably intimidated by an intelligent woman. If a man has an MBA and a woman has an MBA, he isn't going to be intimidated.

The truth of the matter is that men are intimidated by a woman's beauty. A guy will see a beautiful woman that he is physically attracted to and won't say a word to her. Even if he really wants to date her, he'll be too intimidated to talk to her or ask her out. If you think about some of your experiences with men, I'm sure you've been out and seen a guy looking at you, but he never said a word. You wanted him to, but he never had the courage. He is intimidated by your beauty and anticipates you having a man, so to avoid rejection he avoids you. Intimidation equals rejection. If a guy is engaged in a conversation with you and you are talking about your career and how much you know, he's not intimidated.

If men are not intimidated by a woman's intelligence and power, then why aren't they attracted to you and how do you win? First, be attractive physically. Have well-groomed hair, clothes, nails, and shoes. Be emotionally attractive, happy, upbeat, interesting, and smart. Don't talk about the stock market or your number of shares in Yahoo. Lead the conversation to the man – women talk, not business to business conversation. You don't have to prove you are smart or that you are as good as a man. Whoever you are will come across with no extra effort on your part. What he needs is for you to be yourself, loving, nurturing, and beautiful. Tell him what and how you like to take care of your man. You have to sell yourself as the best deal in town. At the end of the day when you two are lying in bed, nude looking at each other your career goals won't matter to him. Either you are connected with each other on a truthful level or you're not.

Some women are intimidated and insecure and feel the need to prove how much they know to woo a man. This comes out of fear that a man won't accept her for who she is. They believe that if they act as a sexy, feminine woman they will somehow be thought of as weak. Sexy, feminine, and smart is the total package; it's very strong. The beauty of being a woman is that for a man, there is only one place to get feminine spiritual energy and that is from a woman. That loving mothering energy is what men want. Men can get the business news and sports scores from his buddies, but his buddies can't give him the touch of a woman.

On a date with a well educated woman with an MBA and working on her PhD, I felt as if I were a guest on Jeopardy. The more she talked, the less attractive she became because her intellect didn't fulfill my needs. Had she invited me over for some homemade lasagna and a movie, I would have loved it. Needless to say, that relationship never got off the ground. Mimi is smart; she didn't talk about her job with Jake. Had she, he too would have been turned off and bored. Instead she did talk and show him how she would please him. That turned Jake on. Men receive so much rejection from women on a daily basis. To receive some attention, some acceptance, and willingness to please is what every man dreams of.

Online Dating

Similarly, these same rules apply to online dating in the sense that women need to know what gets men's attention and what men are looking for. Here is a real ad from an online dating site. This ad is characteristic of most ads – *Women Seeking Men*. In this ad she inevitably describes what she is seeking. Seldom does an ad states what she wants to give. To put it in other words, her ad read like what's in it for me and not how can I contribute? How can I help? Granted these online sites have templates where you fill in the blanks or pick between choices one, two, or three. Most online dating sites let you write your profile and describe what you are looking for.

The ad reads: 28 YEAR OLD FEMALE SEEKING A MAN - *I'm pretty much a fun, down to earth, happy, open-minded girl, looking to meet some fun, interesting people with the potential for a meaningful relationship!! I want to meet someone who is not a bump on the log, enjoys life, grounded, well-rounded, cultured, attractive (to me), honest, loyal, funny, giving, educated, enjoys traveling, dining, outdoors and has good values (BIG PLUS if you also from the east coast, i.e. New York). Am I asking for too much??? Originally from the Boston area, moved to the west coast 2 years ago and have lived here in San Francisco and Hawaii. I have good family values; strong family and friend ties back east and miss them so much. But I love the beach, nice weather and Cali-lifestyle; however, I also require a bit of the city life. This is my first time online wanting to meet some quality guys because I ain't meeting them in the bars, so let's see how this goes!!!*

In her ad she never mentions how she wants to please a man. Most women are saying basically the same thing – what's in it for me – versus how can I help. Apart from not motivating a man, her ad reads like all the rest. Of course she should say what she is looking for, but in her online ad and in her personal profile there is an opportunity for her to express what she can bring to a relationship – not what's in it for her.

Understand your chocolate's fundamental needs – certainty, uncertainty, significance, connection, growth, and contribution. If you give him too much certainty he will be bored. Give him some uncertainty; it's the chase that he is addicted too. Also, uncover where myths about relationships originate. For instance, little girls are taught over and over again that a knight in shining armor will arrive at their doorstep. These storytellers, moms, teachers, aunts, and grandmothers have never experienced that knight. If society is going to sell a romantic idea, make it clear that it is a romantic idea and not a reality. The reality of obtaining a knight in shining armor takes skills, especially if you want chocolate.

Solid Milk Chocolate ~

"Chocolate is the best when it melts so creamy and soft in your mouth and it slides down your throat." Anonymous

Defining a Relationship

Fundamentally, what is a relationship between a man and woman? A relationship is two strangers who spend a given length of time together getting to know each other, sometimes for the better, other times with the intention of being for the better, but it turns out for the worse. If you are in a marriage, then you have chosen to spend the rest of your life getting to know your mate. Ironically, as you get to know your partner, better than 50% of the country ends up divorced.

Whether you are dating or married, you don't completely know the person you are with. Even in our deepest loving relationships, what your partner exposes to you is his superficial layers that he wants you to see, not who he really is. The layers we hide are sometimes physical and/or emotional. Mimi and Jake met as strangers, each hiding their true layers. Jake pretends or believes he is the committed type. In the beginning Mimi pretends she doesn't need a relationship. Not until the relationship peaks does each stranger, Mimi and Jake, reveal their true selves. Then both are shocked by the results.

Mimi ultimately wanted more. She wanted Jake and her to be "One." You don't become "One" in a marriage or a dating relationship. You are two separate adult individuals who agree to share space, time, energy, and emotions with each other - that's all. The energy and time that is spent between two people in love is for their own selfish reasons. They might need the attention of another person, they don't like being alone, or they enjoy serving another person. These arrangements come with positive and negative emotions. When your heart and emotions are involved with these strangers we no longer see them as strangers, but as lovers, husbands, wives, best friends, boyfriends and fiancés. These titles don't entitle you access to really know this person. There are only titles to help us define our feelings and commitments. At the end of the day, they are still strangers that you are getting to know or don't care to know anymore.

When the relationship ends, isn't it ironic how your lover, husband, wife, best friend, boyfriend, or fiancé are put back into the category of stranger or even worse, the asshole stranger? During the happy times in your relationship you two are naked all the time – kissing - having sex – showering together, the whole nine. After the breakup, your ex comes over as you are getting out of the shower. You cover your body as if the cable man arrived too early. You don't feel comfortable with your ex seeing you naked, even though he has seen you nude a thousand times.

When you see someone walking down the street, you see them as a stranger and vice versa. When these two strangers meet, they don't magically become "One" and they don't magically know each other just because they make it to the altar and say

"I do." Sometimes we see strangers and are fearful because they look suspicious. As he walks past you, you clutch your purse and he thinks to himself, "What a snob." The very same suspicious character and the snob that walked past each other a half hour ago can become friends when they see each other at their mutual friend's house party. Although they have become friends, they are still strangers.

Mitch (25) and Deanna (24) have been dating for three years. For twenty-two years, neither knew the other existed. They might have stood next to each other in a crowded elevator or in line at the grocery store, but never spoke because they were two complete strangers. During the twenty-two years prior to meeting, Mitch and Deanna both experienced life and gained information that makes them who they are. This is an incredible amount of experiences, knowledge, wisdom, fears, pain, anger, laughter, confidence, insecurities, and self-awareness. As destiny would have it, they met and then started down the path of dating and getting to know each other. At the same time, they are simultaneously growing and experiencing life daily at work and throughout their given day.

To really get to know someone in the most intimate way it would probably take that number of years of that person's life. In Mitch and Deanna's case it would take twenty-two years to get to know their first twenty-two years. At the same time they would have to keep up with the rate at which the other grows on a daily basis.

Everyone has secrets they will never ever share with their partner. On the physical side it could be your past sexual experiences. It is highly improbable that a woman would ever tell her man about all of her past encounters and what happened during those encounters. Besides, most guys really don't want to know. They would rather you keep your sexual encounters to yourself. Nevertheless, if asked, she will conveniently forget to tell her man about the warm summer night in South Beach, Florida, that lasted until the sun came up. Surely she won't share with him how she really earned her Girls Gone Wild beads or her fantasy about the firemen in the neighborhood. At the same time, the guy is tight lipped about an encounter with a woman he is too embarrassed to mention or the night he was lonely and made an in-call massage appointment that led to a happy ending. These are only a few physical events that happen in our lives that we don't share.

What about the emotional secrets? Do we dare to share them? Who would confess they have low self-esteem as a result of abusive parents? Most of us do our best to act the opposite. Who wants to share the family secret, especially if you are the secret? Do you really know your partner and do they really know you? Instead of saying, "I know that person," say, "I'm getting to know more about the person I choose to be with for the rest of my life." That way you don't have unrealistic expectations about them or yourself.

Because we are always evolving and receiving information, it is not practical to enter a relationship looking for your potential partner to be the "The One." Nor, is it practical to treat your life like a theatrical play, casting for the male lead role of your husband. You and your partner will grow and be influenced on a daily basis by friends, the media, and life's every day challenges.

Let's suppose you really wanted to get to know everything about your partner. You would have to keep up with each other's growth pace. They would have to start from their earliest memory. You two would spend the majority of your time talking about how each of you is influenced every day. Who does that and who would want to do that? With our busy lives, we barely talk with one another as it is. Enjoy each other and your time evolving together. The fun of a relationship is getting to know the person anyway. Be okay with not knowing your partner 100% or knowing the number of women he's been with. He's not going to tell you anyway and you sure aren't going to tell him your little secrets.

Love

Love is the greatest drug ever created, capable of incredible highs and lows. It's powerful, addictive, engrossing, fascinating, distracting, and amorous. It feels good and bad at the same time. Life and death has depended on it. Love can make you sick to the point where you literally stop eating. You lose weight, and abandon your priorities as we saw with Mimi. Most songs that are written are about love: love lost, love gained, and love unrequited. Men have built monuments because of their endless love. Some women have put their careers aside due to love and others put their children second to love. Love is by far the most dominant drug in the world.

I believe that of all things mankind has an abundance of that there is an unlimited supply of love to give. I don't believe anyone has ever said on their death bed, "I have no more love to give." It seems to me that the more love we give, the more love we have to give. To say we as humans have an abundance of love is an understatement. This is especially true when love comes from your spiritual side.

Of the many characteristics mankind has, one of the most prevailing is the insatiable need to give that which they have an abundance of. Whether it is a plethora of wealth or information; the rich become philanthropists, the educator writes books, the entrepreneurs teach the secrets of success, and abundance of information is shared on the Internet. The giving and the sharing of love is no exception.

Unfortunately, our modern societal conditioning contradicts our natural human need to love someone unconditionally in a committed intimate relationship. In our relationship with the one we love, there are invisible boundaries that won't allow us to give them unconditional love nor receive love in abundance, i.e. Jake and Mimi. The reason is that there is the physical you, which is susceptible and easy prey to negative triggers, the triggers that prevent you from receiving love in abundance. These triggers are planted in you during your formative years by your parents, school, church, friends, and/or family. Then there is the spiritual you (your soul) which is unaffected by life's negative triggers and has unlimited love to give. The physical and the spiritual you are in conflict when it comes to love.

When we love, we love from either the physical self or the spiritual self. The reason a mother, a philanthropist, or a teacher can love over and over again unconditionally is because the love comes, from their spiritual self. There is no physical attachment – its non sexual. When the spiritual you loves your pet or when you love your nephew it is a different love than the one you give your boyfriend.

Your child or children are not strangers to *you;* you know them better than you know yourself. You know them quite well from the time they are born to about thirteen years of age when they begin to have their own lives and secrets. They are the only people you'll ever really know. It's ironic; think about it – how well do you know your parents, other than the obvious? Do you know your mother or father's favorite colors? What makes them truly happy or sad? What they dream about or their sexual history, fantasies or desires? And when it comes to our parent's intimate love life most of us don't want to know, which tells me we really don't know our parents.

Not knowing the difference between loving your boyfriend, husband, lover, or significant other spiritually vs. physically will surely lead to relationship failure. Again, because the spiritual you is non-conditioned; therefore, you can love and give love unconditionally. The physical you is conditioned by social factors; therefore, unfortunately you have to return love with conditions – based on our **level 2** upbringing.

Love can also be transitory. When love is lost and you move on to another relationship, the significance you gave your now ex-partner disappears. Feelings are gone or decrease and that person is a memory in your past. We start the process of getting to know a new stranger all over again. You share long phone conversations, Valentine's Day dinner, visiting your could be in-laws and coming up with cute pet names for each other. Of course you never want to be called the pet names from your ex's, unless it's the generic names of *Honey, Baby, Sweetheart, Babe, or Boo.* The new partner, whom you didn't know a year ago, is now your significant other with all the emotions attached. The previous month they didn't exist in your memory, nor did you have any emotional ties. Now you claim you are "One" or he is "The One!"

Take the stress and the expectations out of your relationship by accepting the reality that you don't have to be soul mates with each other to be happy or in love. Once you stop looking for him to be "The One," you'll see that your relationship will begin to have new life as you see each other more objectively or as separate individuals. When you see each other's separate strengths and weaknesses, your communication with each other will open up for the better. You are honest and exposing who you really are, not living the idea that you both should have equal and identical needs and desires.

If you met someone tomorrow that you were very interested in, you would ask questions to get to know the person better. The same is true in long-term committed relationships. Think of each day as if it were the first day you met. Simply ask your partner questions, such as how does he feel about turning thirty? What are his fears today that he didn't have last year? What can I do to be a better friend? These types of questions and communication will help you see that you are not "One" and that there is a lot you don't know about each other. You also learn that you, your relationship, and your man are always evolving. Asking questions and being non-judgmental about their answers will make them share more. Getting to know your partner will keep you connected. The more you share with each other, the closer you will become. The closer you become, the greater the communication, the greater the communication, the stronger the connection. The more connected you are, the more intimate you will be with each other. In addition, when someone shares their intimate feelings and/or secrets, it's not for you to use against them in the future; that is a no no.

The Assumption

Seasoned couples shut down communication by assuming. Assuming they know their partner and assuming they know the outcome of a given situation. When a couple goes to bed at night, they already think they know the outcome. He does this, she does that, and we fall asleep. Boring! Boring! Boring! Granted, I know you are tired, you have kids, it was a long day, you have to get up early, he isn't being romantic, etc. I know all the side effects of romance, but if you are feeling the exact same way (tired or sleepy) and by chance that night you meet your dream man, I am certain you'll put all the excuses aside and stay up all night showing him the time of his life. Then wake up the next day perky as can be, as if you had twelve hours worth of sleep. If you are single and reading this you know exactly what I'm talking about.

What is the difference between sex with your boyfriend / husband and the guy you just met? The difference is you stop communicating with your boyfriend / husband because you really think you know this person and start assuming. With the new stranger in your life, you literally don't know him; therefore, you can't assume. You want to get to know him and vice versa. You want to capture his heart and attention. You are afraid to assume and take things for granted because he might leave or you might be wrong. To keep his interest you show him a good time.

Remember those marathon phone conversations that lasted 'til 2AM. You ask each other what do you like? What is the wildest thing you've ever done? What turns you on? Have you ever been with a female and would you ever? You asked each other all the questions to help move a potential relationship forward. How many times in the beginning of your relationship did you agree with your guy when he said for example – I love camping outdoors and you said, "Wow, me too!" Then the both of you added a mental hash mark next to your list of things you have in common. The more you have in common the more you feel a connection and you can't wait to jump each other's bones. The reason this works so well is because you don't assume. The times you do make assumptions you are not really interested in the relationship.

Seasoned couples that make assumptions have an outcome that is headed for trouble. Two years ago when you met there were many things that at the time you felt one way and today you feel a different way. It could be your views, values, moral beliefs, political beliefs, love, money, racism, cancer, sex, food, diet, environment, war and peace, and so on. During the two years or at any time, one category can influence the other. A young woman close to you is diagnosed with breast cancer and could possibly die within a year or two. Her cancer makes you realize just how short our time on Earth really is and that any moment could be our last. This realization makes you rethink many aspects of your life. For one, you no longer want to be a sexual prude and want to live out your desires today and stop waiting for tomorrow. Maybe you become a vegetarian because you believe it will give you better health. You know you live a preventative lifestyle all because your friend has cancer.

Many things and events can change our outlook and behavior on a daily basis over time. It could be a friend, the news, family, the weather, or your own maturity. Whatever and however you are influenced, change is going to happen to you and your partner throughout your relationship. So why assume you know your partner or the outcome. In your relationship should you assume? Should you go to bed and assume the outcome based on what you believe your partner wants and who your partner is today, compared to two years ago? You are lying in bed assuming your partner is still into XYZ and comes to find out he is now into WXYZ. It takes two to tango – it's not solely your responsibility, but it's your responsibility to yourself. If your man is lazy and wants to have routine sex, ask him what is he really into now? What does he feel about sex today that he didn't feel in the past? Then share your feeling. The safer and non-judgmental we are about our wants and desires the more he will open up. Your man might have a foot fetish and is afraid to mention it out of fear of rejection. Two years earlier he mentioned it and you frowned upon it. Today you are turned on by his foot fetish, but neither of you talk about it. We are all interesting people, so why not explore who we are and who we want to become with ourselves and our partner. Don't assume that your partner's needs haven't changed from two years ago or even two weeks ago. Our wants are constantly changing as we mature and grow. Talk. Ask questions to get to know your partner better.

Stop window shopping for "The One" – he doesn't exist. There are as many "Ones" as there are strangers in the world. If you meet someone that you want to commit a certain amount of time of your life to, see them, for who they are, not who you wish them to be. You meet a cute guy and immediately your imagination starts running wild. Within two minutes of meeting him, you see him as the father of your children and you're thinking, "My parents are going to like him." Just stop it. He is a stranger who might want to be in a relationship with you. If he does choose to be with you, you have some work cut out for you before he is ready for Mom and Dad. You two are from different worlds and getting to know each other is going to take some time. We are all strangers to each other living in a civilized society where we agree to love and care about each other in the most civil way.

Sugar Free Chocolate ~

"Life is like a box of chocolates - you never know what you're going to get." Forrest Gump in "Forrest Gump" (1994)

Your Soul Mate!

Mimi and Jake felt like soul mates when they were together. They felt so good it is hard for them to imagine being apart. They were "One." Much like the ideal of "The One," I don't believe in the ideal of soul mates. I have searched for the meaning of the term soul mate. To be quite honest, I couldn't find a believable definition or concrete idea that leads me to believe that such people exist. For one thing, in your lifetime you can love many people or be in love with more than one person. Most people do fall in love several times over their lifetime. Two, according to the *American Heritage Dictionary*

Soul mate
n. *One of two persons compatible with each other in disposition, point of view, or sensitivity.*

One or two persons compatible with each other! That doesn't sound like some spiritual connection that you need to search throughout your life to find; seeking an elusive person that you'll drive yourself crazy searching for. According to the *American Heritage Dictionary* definition, a soul mate can be a co-worker, a best friend, or family, and not necessarily a boyfriend, lover or husband. By definition, you are more likely to find your soul mate in a best friend or family member than a stranger. Because without the emotional and physical attachment to the relationship, it is easier to find a compatible disposition, point of view and sensitivity with a friend than a lover, husband, or boyfriend. Once you add sex to any relationship, you change the relationship dynamic. Your emotions and issues will surface and now both are going to disagree on different points of view, all because you had sex. The emotional attachments to sex will always surface and what seemed like a soul mate in the beginning becomes another average relationship. It is the emotional thoughts and feelings that make you believe that you have found your soul mate. This is only evident in the very beginning of your relationship – which is better explained in the chapter *Filling in the Gap*. In addition, if there really were soul mates wouldn't the divorce rate be much lower than 50%?

I'm not stating that there are not couples that are great together. Yes, there are some who seem to be consistently compatible with each other in disposition, point of view, and sensitivity. It doesn't mean they are soul mates. What I am suggesting is that chasing after your elusive soul mate puts unnecessary and unrealistic expectations on yourself and your potential life partner. I understand the feeling of being with your chocolate. It makes you feel like you are soul mates that you are a match made in heaven.

One of the reasons for wanting our own soul mate comes from observing couples that appear perfect to us and the outside world. They look happy and satisfied. It is in our human nature to want the same. Meeting these happy and in love couples naturally makes us believe; we want that same feeling. We want someone we can lean on, someone to kiss and love, that special someone to spend the holidays and special occasions with. We say, "I want my soul mate." "Men of my past were not my soul mate, I settled - never again." The woman you see being kissed as her man embraces her doesn't seem as though she settled and you think she got exactly what you want – a soul mate.

No matter how fantastic couples look to the outside world, their relationships go through the same up and down cycles of any relationship. Those that claim to have found their soul mate disagree, argue, and complain just as much as couples who accept each other as strangers that are getting to know each other better. The depth to which the soul mates love one another (excluding the first thirty days of their relationship) isn't any greater or lesser than the couple next door that fights with each other once a week. At least the couple next door is venting their frustration and getting their feelings out. We confuse the feelings of the first thirty days with having found a soul mate.

Another way the idea of soul mates is sold to single people is through films, television, and romance novels. They paint fairytales stories that are a heartwarming ideology that we all need to find our soul mates to be happy. This is not a jab at the entertainment media. It's actually a brilliant idea because we are all taught that we need a soul mate and how bad we need it. We are taught there is one special person out there for us in the world and if we are lucky we'll find them – as seen as topics on talk shows.

For instance, a woman watching a television talk show listens to a celebrity couple named Jim and Jessica. She listens to them tell how they are made for each other. Jessica says Jim makes her whole, and that he is so amazing, and she can't live without him. He is indeed the only man for her and she couldn't be happier. These are romantic thoughts that sound too good to be true and they are misleading. As great of a guy as Jim is to Jessica, it doesn't mean they don't argue, disagree, have resentful feelings, are jealous or have some insecure feelings about their relationship. It also doesn't mean that they don't have incompatible dispositions, point of views, or sensitivities at times. No one ever questions what happened to the couple who is now divorced, but years earlier claimed they had found their soul mates and announced to the world their undying love. What happened to them being soul mates?

We all have our share of childhood insecurities that we carry into our adult life. These insecurities don't go away because you have found your soul mate. If a young girl's father is seldom at home as Mimi's dad is, she will someday fall in love with a guy she calls her soul mate. Over time, the impression her father made on her of being emotional unavailable will creep into her relationship with her soul mate. How it happens depends on the couple's relationship. One way it might show up is when he leaves the house for work or play. The moment he walks out the door her trigger from fifteen years ago switches on and now she accuses her soul mate of not caring about her and being selfish. Naturally, he will react to her and there goes the idea of a soul mate – a couple who fights and argues like the rest of the world.

Just because you are soul mates doesn't mean that your issues won't cause conflict in your relationship, thus the high divorce rate. Besides, you only see half the story. In romance novels and chick flicks you see what the writer and director wants you to believe. They want you to believe that in *Pretty Woman* two strangers from completely different backgrounds find their soul mates in each other. How often does a millionaire date prostitutes without major complications? Remember the prostitute is definitely a **Level 2,** she is Jake. *Pretty Woman* and other similar stories leave out the other half. Just as you see a couple holding hands and kissing; it's only half the story. Also, of all the couples that you personally know including family, extended family, friends, acquaintances, celebrity couples, and romance novel characters, you should want their relationship. If you do your homework there shouldn't be one relationship you would want to trade with. The other half of the story you don't hear about is that their relationship isn't managed as well as yours. Those people you know the full story about such as your sister's relationship with her husband or your best friend's relationship – the odds are you wouldn't want to trade places with them. Don't beat yourself up and want to trade places with any couple or envy their relationship. Anyone who saw Mimi and Jake at the beginning of their relationship would envy them, but near the end you would run the other way and tell Mimi she could do better than Jake.

Don't let these and other concepts of finding your soul mate be used as an excuse for you to be single. As virtuous as "I'm waiting for Mr. Right, my soul mate" or "I'm not going to settle, I'm a good person with a ton of love to give" may sound, don't let it become a lame excuse to be single. If you want to be in a relationship you should be in a relationship. The truth of the matter is, *no one settles for less.* <u>You are only with the partner you and your self-esteem feels you deserve.</u> If you really believe that you deserve more, you would have more. Look at other personal choices in your life and see if you are settling or getting what you deserve. The person who gets an MBA feels they deserve a higher salary than a person who is content with a B.A. degree salary. The person who is in great shape feels they deserve to look the best they can. The point being that people who feel they deserve more work more to achieve that goal. The high school dropout can say they deserve more and won't settle for any job. I can assure you they will be waiting their lifetime for the high paying job they think they deserve.

If you've dated an unemployed musician and after you broke up you say, "I've settled," you didn't settle you chose him. He chose you because you both believed at that time it is the best you could do. You've heard the expression water seeks its own level?

When it comes to soul mates, do you personally know any couples that are soul mates? Is the concept of soul mates exclusive only to the chosen few? Are soul mates exclusive to a certain age group, ethnicity, economic background, or geographical area? Is everyone entitled to a soul mate or are we wasting time and spinning our wheels looking for that perfect partner? Are we letting people with great partner potential slip right by us? Most people don't participate in their lives – they sit on the sidelines of life and watch, waiting for Mr. Right to knock. Be pro-active and develop the relationship you want. Do the necessary work you would need to get the right job, and anticipate there are going to be relationship challenges.

20 Years – 40 Dates

I think women let too many good men slip through their fingers and then complain there aren't any worthy men available. They have set unrealistic expectations for themselves and the potential relationship they seek. Take an average forty-year-old single, working woman with average looks. Being conservative, let's say she started dating at the age of twenty and for the next twenty years until she is forty years old she dates two men a year for a total of forty intimate relationships. Of course some women are in relationships for three years, or eight, or ten, etc. Nevertheless, in a twenty year span she has probably dated, if not met, more than twenty men. I'm not even including one night stands, the numerous dates she turned down, or the men that have passed through her life. Of all the men she has encountered over twenty years, there wasn't one or two or five men she could have developed a relationship with and married? It is hard to believe that she didn't have the opportunity to be in a loving committed relationship. When I meet women that are single in their late thirties or forties the majority of the time they certainly haven't learned how to manage their chocolate. Just as important, they tend to be looking for the better deal, "The One," or their elusive soul mate. For this reason they are single today. I know there are women who have only been with two guys in twenty years or been married for fifteen years. Whatever your history, you've met many men. You did your best to make a dying situation work. Regardless, do your homework today so that you don't let another potential partner slip away.

The reason I mention the idea of soul mates and finding one is because we like to romanticize about relationships and not see them for what they are, but what we want them to be. If you are the type that is looking for your soul mate, you'll be looking a long time. Soul mate or not, relationships take the same amount of work. How is it possible for Jennifer Smith from New York and Steve Jackson from Houston to be soul mates? They were both raised with different values, morals, and influences. It is difficult enough to live with your own siblings who grew up with the same parents, religion, morals, and values. How do complete intimate strangers make for perfect soul mates? Change your expectations and don't expect the person you choose to be your knight in shining armor, but rather a stranger, someone whom you choose to build a productive relationship with. No man will ever live up to your fantasy man. Men come with their own set of issues and imperfections, just like you. Ask your girlfriend to describe her ideal man. Listen closely as she describes him and ask yourself have you ever seen that guy. When you read the online dating profile – women seeking men – you can read how unrealistic women can be.

Some people feel that when you put effort in your relationship, romance is lost. If you tell your partner what you really desire and how you want things, romance isn't lost, in fact romance is gained. Sharing your wants and needs will bring you closer together. Had Mimi and Jake been able to communicate what they realistically needed and expected of each other, their relationship would have had a better chance of success. Whenever you can be honest with anyone it will bring you closer together, provided you are not being judged or reprimanded for your honesty. When you don't feel you are being judged, it allows you to open up emotionally and physically. Intimate honesty will give your love life an opportunity to grow and you'll feel the need to please each other as best as you can. As for yourself, you'll feel more confident that you can please him any day of the week now that you know what he wants and how he wants it. No more guessing what he like or dislikes and vice versa.

I was speaking with a woman who said she is "Looking for a guy that knew exactly what she wanted." She felt he should know what and how she wanted things without needing to ask. I asked her, "Are you serious?" She replied, "Yes." I said, "Why do you feel this way?" She said, "If he really loved me or cared then he should just know." Think about it, isn't that crazy and unrealistic, yet common. How can anyone demand another person to be a soul mate or at the very least behave like one?

If you are a parent, or imagine being a parent, you are going to give your child unconditional love with no strings attached. You'll love them more than any other person in your life. Every day you are going to do your best to be a better parent. You'll want to cook better, communicate better, be a better teacher, and love them better. Does the work you put into making your child's life better diminish the thrill of being a parent? If you are not a parent, you have experienced your own parents, whom over the years have never lost their passion to love you more each day. In fact, as you grow older you realize how much they love you and are committed to you. You don't love them any less and neither do they. The same is true for your relationship. The more you practice communicating and sharing your needs, being a great sexual partner, and so forth, the more you'll love the challenge of being in a relationship. It is when you stop growing that love can be lost.

As you get to know your partner and share experiences, you'll find that this is what makes love grow and brings you closer. It is not some notion that you are a going to meet your soul mate when you least expect it as you take a train ride from Paris to London. Keep your expectations for your chocolate real for the sake of yourself and him. Soul mate or not, use your time together to get to know each other. Stay alert in your relationship by asking probing questions that will bring you closer to this stranger and not assume the outcome.

Chocolate (Hershey's) Kisses ~

"Chemically speaking, chocolate really is the world's perfect food." Michael Levine, nutrition researcher, as quoted in "The Emperors of Chocolate: Inside the Secret World of Hershey and Mars". *Anonymous*

Mother – Son Effect

MOTHERS INFLUENCE - Most mothers teach their sons how to be Mr. Nice Guys or at least want them to be the nice guys. She tells him not to be mean to girls, not to play rough with them, and for him to be sure to bring an apple to his teacher. Isn't it ironic that she teaches him to be the very man that she is least attracted to? Why would she want her son to grow up to be Bob? Shouldn't she want him to be the man that women are more attracted to, i.e. George Clooney or Johnny Depp? Wouldn't this give him the largest pool of women to choose from? When I see these examples I ask, is mom living out a romance fantasy vicariously through her son about what she dreams men should be? Does she really know the reality between the sexes? Is it that she can't bear the thought of her son being Jake and wants him to be Bob? In either case, her advice is filled with irony and contradictions, because she loves her chocolate just as much as the next woman. When mothers inadvertently give these values to their sons, ultimately mothers are doing them a disservice when it comes to girls.

Little girls are taught three basic things about men that are contrary to what males are taught 1) Men are dogs 2) All men want is sex 3) Men can't be trusted. These values are in direct conflict with what boys are taught, especially guys like Bob who are looking for validation from women like Mimi. Males are taught to respect women whether they deserve respect or not. Be nice to women. Be a gentleman.

Preferably, the son should be taught behaviors that will assist him in being the best partner. He shouldn't be taught to respect every woman, just because she is a female. As with everyone, respect is something that has to be earned. He should be taught that women are more emotional and less logical. Women prefer to be held or have some sort of connection after sex with a man, rather than him having sex and immediately leaving. Young girls should be taught that men have many great qualities.

The mother is the first and most influential female relationship that a man will ever have. She is given the huge responsibility of influencing him with her values on countless aspects of life: food, fashion, money, sex, law, education, religion, and racism. More importantly, his confidence and self-esteem also depends on her. Other important values he is taught is how he perceives love; giving and receiving. Is his mother affectionate and attentive? Is she emotionally unavailable and critical of her son's sense of self-worth? Is she a builder of his block of cheese or will she slowly chisel it away throughout his life? Whatever the case, her character will sway his behavior to that of Jake – pure milk chocolate or Bob – simple green salad and ideally a combination of them both. And yes, dads have a major and important role in the development of their sons, but for now I'm speaking about the mother-son relationship.

Because the mother's influence is perpetual and permanent, it becomes his blueprint that defines who and what he becomes and which type of woman will find him most challenging and compatible. If the mother is uncompassionate and uninvolved in a boy's life, generally speaking, he'll seek that type of woman for companionship. The same is true if his mother is passionate and loving. He'll most likely seek a compassionate woman as his companion. Of course, there are mothers who are a blend of both varieties. Consciously or subconsciously, a mother teaches her son what love is or is not.

Ironically, a man raised by a mother who is emotionally unavailable might allege he wants a compassionate caring woman. When he conjures up Ms. Loving and Ms. Available, i.e. the Mimi in this life, he is eventually bored with that relationship or he can't handle that type of attention. He then yearns for an emotional challenge the same way Mimi yearned for Jake when she is dating Bob. It is also the same challenge that stood between Jake and his mother's love.

Most of us are taught that love is something you compete for. When Ms. Loving meets her chocolate, it seems as though the attention and care is what he really needs. Over time – thirty days or so, you'll see that he won't be able to handle the attention she gives because of the two incompatible impulses. On one hand, he welcomes her attention because he needs it. On the other hand, he pushes it away as if it's toxic. His rubber band – back and forth reactions – are frustrating and confusing for her. It's no fault of his, he doesn't know any different.

If Jake's mother were very nurturing and caring, he would never be bored by the constant attention of love and affection from Mimi. Since we are all victims of the black box – white box theory, Mimi eventually bores Jake. If alternatively Jake were to give her excessive amounts attention, by comparison to what she received from her father, she would get bored; consequently, the negative relationship cycle between the sexes.

You can avoid this common cycle, of meeting a guy, opening your heart to him, only to be dumped, meeting another guy, opening up your heart, then being dumped again and again. Simply follow the blueprint that mothers instill on their sons. She has laid the ground work that he, almost without a choice, now lives by.

Some women want to create a new blueprint on their man; they want to change him. Sometimes it's defined as a rescue mission. They are going to save their chocolate from himself and show him the ways of the more responsible and reliable lifestyle. Alternatively, they take a Bob and change his Ivy League style, and make him wear designer jeans with the hope he'll develop a bad boy edge; it ain't gonna happen.

If you think you want to change your man's blueprint from what his mother has given him, think again. Creation is easier said than done for three reasons - 1) Who wants to be changed? 2) Who is willing to change? 3) It is very difficult to impossible to change one's childhood blueprint.

Have you ever dated a man that you were crazy about? Then one day you wake up and decide the way he is just isn't good enough? You just weren't 100 % satisfied so you thought you would change him? Did it work? Have you ever dated a guy and he tells you in so many words he wants you to change? It could be your hairstyle or the way you walk or talk? Did you change for him? Have you been in a situation where a guy likes you and no matter what, there is nothing he can say or do to change your blueprint from being friends to lovers?

We all modify our behavior, but to change the core of what we are, it's not going to happen and we like what we like. FYI – In our attempt to change someone, we believe they will benefit from our advice we believe that they can and will live a better quality life. I believe the real drive to change another person only serves our own selfish needs. If we don't want to change or be changed, why should we expect someone would want to change for us. Changing your man or rescuing your man isn't about the kindliness of your heart as much as it is about your need to feel needed. The things we don't like in others, we do not like in ourselves.

Mimi wanted to change Jake. The mistake Mimi made is she didn't know how to follow Jake's mother's blueprint. If he wasn't raised by his mother, but another female or male figure, the rules would still apply. Follow mom's blueprint. If he were raised by his father because the mother abandoned him or she passed away when he was two years old, he doesn't have a sense of closeness to women. He'll feel uncomfortable with a lot of intimacy or will have trust issues. If you want to change someone, they have to be intelligent and motivated, and you have to have emotional leverage. Unless it's your child, it is very difficult to accomplish. Not impossible, but difficult. Then you have to ask the question, what's the point of changing someone? Why not choose someone who has the majority of the qualities you want and accept the rest.

Some of you might think to yourself, "I don't want to be his mother or compete with the mother." I'm not suggesting that you compete or play the role of his mother, but clearly the triggers of our influences are established in our childhood. If you want your relationship to work in your favor, just follow the patterns, they are there to serve you.

How do we know what the patterns or blueprints are? The easiest way to understand his history with his mother is to ask him. Ask him specific questions. As a kid was your mother nurturing? Did she attend all of your sporting events? Did she make dinner every night? Does she talk to you without being judgmental? Is she affectionate? Have him give you examples. I can assure you, you'll really see the true relationship between him and his mom. Beware – if your chocolate grows up with a mean mother, you are going to feel compelled to save him. Don't be Mimi. Stick to the rules.

My favorite question to ask is, "Does your mother know your favorite color?" The answer is usually no. My other favorite question is, Which way do you feel most loved by your mother: being held, being told, being shown, or looked in the eyes? I believe when a parent doesn't know specific details about their child's likes and dislikes, such as their favorite color, movie, song, or goals, it says a lot about the intimacy between the parent and the child; If the answer is "No, my mother doesn't know my favorite color." Usually this is a telltale sign that he is more similar to a Jake than a Bob.

Unfortunately, parents usually only know the answers to such intimate questions as what is your favorite color, favorite song, or favorite time of day, up until about the age of thirteen. After thirteen, the child becomes more independent and parents tend to lose that level of intimacy with their child. The child wants autonomy and wants to stop sharing personal feelings and personal information. In spite of how a child matures, I think the parent never really asks specific questions to get to know the child on that new intimate level in the first place. The answers to such questions as, what is your favorite color are learned through circumstance. The daughter wants everything pink. A kid will volunteer what their favorite bedtime book is over and over again or request pizza for every meal. Then it becomes obvious what their favorite color is and what food or books they like. For the most part, I don't believe parents intentionally avoid asking those questions, I think they take the relationship for granted and assume they know their child on that intimate level.

It has been my experience with children that they get a great sense of connection when you ask the simple questions such as - What is your favorite color. What is your favorite time of day; and so on? There is also a strong connection when you ask your man those same questions. You'll be amazed how connected the both of you will feel. It's a level of communication intimacy we all ignore or take for granted.

Don't scare him away by asking a thousand personal questions on the first date. Slowly introduce these questions. If you are too direct and ask too many personal questions, he might close up and not be honest, but who wouldn't! Sometimes we all can have blurred vision of our past or we aren't very open about our childhood. Therefore, we provide less accurate information about our past. It might a take a while for him to open up and for you to understand the true relationship between him and his mother, if so be patient and listen.

I hope you can see how the mother influences the boy that becomes a man. Follow her pattern and you'll hit those triggers that define your chocolate as love or intimacy and he will find you attractive. It is those same triggers that Mimi learned as a kid and found attractive in Jake.

Loyalty

Another important fact about the mother and son relationship is the loyalty between them.

It's ironic just how loyal they are to each other considering their relationship is not based on intelligence or sexuality. Men have an incredible loyalty to their mothers their entire life and it's rare when a man doesn't. Their loyalty is often tested throughout his life and regardless of the circumstance; their chain of loyalty is never broken. A boy might spend the night at a friend's house and no matter how great his friend's mom treats him, he is unequivocally committed and loyal to his mother. After one night, he is ready to go back home. Often when a boy gets home, the first words out of his mouth are "I miss you, you are the best mommy." His friend's mother might have made the most delicious dinner and desert, yet the son gladly comes home to the world's greatest mom. In his adult relationship he might date some of the most amazing, loving, nurturing, sexual women in the world. At the end of the day his mother is the better deal in the sense of trust, availability, and unwavering loyalty.

You have to give the mother a lot of credit. It is one of the few times that a woman isn't jealous, threatened, or insecure of another woman. There are cases where the mother is jealous of his new woman fearing she is going to take him away from her, but mothers tend to be very secure about their role in their son's life. This is true when her son is between the ages of birth to thirteen years old. Mothers sometimes encourage their sons to spend the night away from home at a friend's house or send him to summer camp. She knows that her son will come home. He will come home not only because he is seven years old and has no other place to go, but because it's a bond, a loyalty that she knows he committed to her. There is nothing the other mom's can do to get in between their commitment. Males make it very clear that their mothers come first in their lives.

In your relationship with the man you love, every insecure feeling, thought, pain, and rejection comes to the surface when you see your man simply engaging in what appears to be an intimate conversation with a woman. Why is it that the mother will let her son spend the night, but you are insecure when he is around another woman? The mother-son relationship is very interesting and there is a lot to be learned from it, so you can manage your own relationship.

One of the main reasons their bond is so strong is because, regardless of what a man does, the mother's guard is down and she is always available to him unconditionally, unlike his relationship with a woman he's dating or is married to. A mother's guard is down for her child and is up for her husband, although, they are married for years. When it comes to her children, specifically her son and no matter what his age, her guard is down or non-existent. A case in point is when a man commits some heinous crime and the reporter interviews his mother. She always says, "I can't believe that is my son; he would never do anything like that," although the surveillance videotape says otherwise. She is still loyal to her belief of who her son is.

The relationship between a mother and son is the purest male relationship she'll ever have. Not even the relationship the mother has with her own father and surely not the relationship she'll have with her husband is greater. With her son she is able to give 100% of herself to him and never feel rejection or insecurity. This is not to say that a son doesn't pout and reject his mother at times. On the spiritual level she feels accepted and safe to love him. This relationship meets all of her needs; certainty, uncertainty, significant, connection, growth, and contribution. This is why it is so easy for a mother to ignore her husband and often times does. Prior to having kids, the husband played the role to have her needs met. The downside is that he probably didn't meet her needs unconditionally like her child does, which makes it that much easier for her to make him a lower priority in the marriage. It's very difficult for a husband to compete with the mother-son relationship. A lot of times a woman doesn't care to lose weight or look after herself after giving birth because her needs are being met by her child. What would be her motivation?

There are some very controlling and smothering mothers who can't stand the thought of their sons in the arm or company of another woman. These mothers sometimes have made him so dependent that he can't seem to do anything for himself; he becomes a breast feeder, if you will. She has crippled him. The mother's own needs over shadow what is in her son's best interest and destroy what could be a potentially good man or a good partner. He becomes that lazy unemployed chocolate.

If their loyalty is not based on intellect and sexuality, what keeps them bonded? Why are marriages or committed relationships so vulnerable and often filled with distrust?

Loyalty and trust between a mother and son is based on her womb energy; literally, a woman's womb. Mothers love their sons from the womb where she carried her child for nine months. The womb is the one of only places a child feels 100% safe and comfortable. Mothers don't love their children from a physical place with hidden agendas or with her power and wealth, unlike adult relationships that are filled with hidden agendas. If a guy has an unwilling woman who he wants to have sex with, he'll say anything to get her to agree. A woman's hidden agenda might be to have a baby with a rich man under the pretense that she loves him, when in fact she wants the hefty child support payments. The mother's love is pure from her womb with no hidden agendas or pretense. Her womb energy is what bonds their relationship.

Womb energy is very important and powerful. Women exchange womb energy with each other all the time. By contrast men don't have this womb energy, but seek it. Looking through *National Geographic* a while ago I saw a photograph of a woman about eight months pregnant lying in a canopy bed, dressed in a Middle Eastern Indian outfit with her belly exposed. Next to her, is another woman dressed similarly sitting in the same bed drawing some tribal design on the pregnant woman's stomach using henna ink. They both seemed relaxed and enjoying each other's company. It is a beautiful photograph and an even more beautiful moment of two women exchanging womb energy. Can you imagine two straight guys in a similar situation? Neither can I.

Other examples are two girls holding hands, dancing together, sleeping in the same bed together, or doing each other's hair. While talking with a female friend the other night, she told me that she just moved and had to share the same bed with her daughter until her new bed and mattress arrives. She said when they sleep together they are wrapped around each other – sharing womb energy. Males don't do these types of activities with each other because there is no need to. There is nothing to be gained. You rarely see a man holding another straight man's hand or combing another guy's hair. There is no womb energy to exchange since we don't have a womb; although the womb is very important to men, more than sex. Yes, the womb is more important to a man than sex.

Every man wants to get back into the womb. Men want the same womb energy from a woman that they received from their mothers when they were children – it's just that simple. Although Jake's mother isn't emotionally available, he still came from her womb.

Have you ever read the children story *Are You My Mommy*? It describes a perfect metaphor for a man and woman's relationship. One day, a little duck hatches from its egg. He looks around, but cannot find his mother. "Where is my mommy?" said the baby duck. "I must go and find her." The baby duck sets out on a journey to find his mother. On his journey the baby duck sees a cow and says, "Are you my mommy?" "Why no, I am not your mommy. I am a cow." Then the baby duck sees a pig and says, "Are you my mommy?" "Why no, I am not your mommy. I am a pig." Then baby duck sees a horse and says, "Are you my mommy?" "Why no, I am not your mommy. I am a horse." Then the baby duck sees a big duck and says, "Are you my mother?" "Why yes, I am your mommy," she answers. "I am so glad you found me." And off they went together for a swim in the pond, and they were very, very happy. *Are You My Mommy? By Carla Dijs*

The baby duck is a man and mother duck is his potential partner. When men sleep around from woman to woman they are looking for their mommy or womb. Not literally, but figuratively speaking, he is looking for the woman who will accept him as his mother has done or he is looking for the architect of his blueprint in a woman. Maybe his mother is around as a kid or he is raised by his grandfather. The fact remains no matter who raised him, he started his life like all of us, in his mother's womb. Does he ever find his mommy? Sometimes he does and other times he doesn't. If he is lucky, he finds his way back to the womb.

The possibility exists that a man has met his mate many times over the years except that the women he's met may have had their guard up to protect themselves emotionally, unlike his mother. The man continues from female to female looking for his mommy, until he finds the one who is like his mother and has her guard down.

Sex serves as a vessel for men to get back to the womb. This is not to say that men only have sex to find their mommy. Sex is a need and a want for men, but when a man is going from female to female he is looking for his mommy, the womb. Once he finds the womb, he is very content and loyal, the same way he is with his mother.

The majority of women have their guards up. If a woman is evolved and clever enough to love unconditionally and has a little knowledge on managing her chocolate with her guard down, her man will most likely be a great loyal partner. I know that it is very difficult and scary for a woman to let her wall down out of a fear of being hurt, but letting your wall down simply means putting your womb energy first – (i.e. spiritual) and your sexuality second – (i.e. physical). Women usually put the sexuality first and womb second. We are all taught that sex is the end all, it isn't, it's your womb.

The Beginning

You've seen a young boy about six years old with his mother at the mall. After a long day of shopping with mom, the tired boy just wants to be held. While sitting on a bench and without a second thought, he falls into his mother's arms. His mother holds him as if he's her most loved jewel on Earth. At that moment, it is neither sexual nor intellectual. This boy is in heaven, receiving all this unconditional love and womb energy from his mother. The boy gets pretty much the same attention from his grandmother, his aunt, his female teachers, and pretty much any female. He is after all a cute boy. With mom, he can get this love often, as much as he wants it, and when he wants it.

This unconditional love / womb energy feels so incredible to a boy that he'll yearn for it for the rest of his life. The best part of it all for the boy is that it took so little effort to receive so much - no candlelight dinners, no flowers, and no phone calls, just the cute adorable smile. Fast-forward to seven years later. This same boy is now thirteen years old. He attends a wedding with his loving mother. She's a little warm and thirsty. In her sweet voice, she asks her son to get her a bottle of water. Being the sweet kid that he is, he brings back five bottles of water - one for his mother and the rest for her four female friends sitting at the same table. He knows that he is going to get five times the womb energy. Sure enough, all the females at the table tell the boy how sweet they think he is. They hug and pinch his cheeks. This kid is in heaven, receiving all this female womb energy. He thinks to himself, "This is easy, I gave them bottled water and in return I got a ton of love." Unfortunately for him, their reaction to his cute behavior reinforces his future title of Mr. Nice Guy, aka Bob.

Ten years later, the boy is now a young twenty-two year old man living on his own and seeking affection, attention, and womb energy from females to whom he is physically attracted. One night he goes to a local nightclub and spots an attractive female. Being the gentleman that he is, he offers her a drink. Her girlfriends standing in the wings give him an inviting glance. He thinks it is womb energy and in turn he buys them a drink as well. The ladies gladly accept the free drinks. Their hidden agenda is to save their money and spend his.

Mr. Nice Guy and the girls engage in light conversation. The bartender serves the drinks. As the clock ticks away, he waits for their validation and their unconditional womb energy. After a while he thinks, "Well maybe they are a little distracted." He calls over the bartender, "Another round of drinks for me and the ladies." His would - be female companions seize the opportunity and makes a toast. He is thinking, "Finally the moment I've been waiting for is here... a thank you, a toast to the man of the hour, to the hottest guy in the bar... to our new friend – something, anything." The ladies raise their glasses. The cute blonde he is most attracted to gives the toast. She said, "To the single life; to hot guys with fast cars ... the night is early and we are just getting started." Her girlfriends all say

"Cheers" and down go the shots of tequila. He is dumbfounded - no thanks, no womb energy, no nothing. Unlike his mother, the girls read his kindness as weakness - a typical Bob; plenty of money, but no game. The ladies are operating from **level 2** and he is operating from **level 1**. When **level 1** meets level **2**, **level 2** wins and annihilates **level 1** every time.

The relationship between a son and his female family members are all operating at **level 1**. From the time a boy is born until his heart is broken, he is taught that a woman will love him unconditionally. Once he enters puberty, the girl he is most interested in will definitely let him know that she is not a **level 1,** but indeed a **level 2**.

When he is first rejected, it starts the Mr. Nice Guy syndrome. Because of his need to get back into the womb, he thinks that maybe with the next girl things will be different. Therefore, he works a little harder to please that girl, and then the next and the next. The more rejection he gets, the harder he works for validation.

Playing Mama

Women fear that they are going to be his mother and not be an equal loving partner, not true. So what you mother him, it's very likely he'll father you. Why is that wrong? At times in relationships, a girl should play the role of mother, sister, lover, and friend. The only role a woman shouldn't play in a relationship is the role of father. When you make your man dinner what role are you playing? Are you a waiter? Are playing the role of the mother? Anytime a woman takes care of a male it is maternal. When you clean up or pick up after him what role are you playing? Are you the maid or the mother? When you listen to his day what role are you playing? Are you the therapist or the mother? It is favorable to repeat or follow the roles his mother already established, the emotional good and bad.

Obviously, there are other factors that affect a relationship, but at the core, men are loyal to their mothers. Therefore, they can be loyal to their partner. If he finds that womb, she will most likely be able to close the deal. By approaching the relationship with her womb energy first, and sex second, she is the type that will want to fill his needs. The mother has cooked, cleaned, bathe, taught, laughed, cried, spent thousands of dollars, and thousands of hours with him. The first breast he ever saw was his mother's and the role between them is very loyal and non-sexual. The lesson in this chapter is that mothers know that the most important thing to her son is her womb energy. Pick up where the mother has left off, as she has done all the work for you. Don't attempt to reinvent his blueprint. He is who he is today, tomorrow, and forever. Besides, you can't love anyone more than they are capable of being loved.

People say, "Ask a man how he treats and feels about his mother, that's how he will treat his woman." I say, "Ask a man how his mother feels about him, that's how you are going to treat your man."

Chocolate Caramel ~

"I never met a chocolate I didn't like." Deanna Troi in Star
Trek: The Next Generation

Why Men Itemize

One of the many behavioral characteristics of the Jakes and
non-Jakes of the world is their need to itemize women's
bodies. Instead of looking at a women's body as a whole, they
find themselves attracted to one specific part of her body. Her
breasts, legs, or lips can be enough to satisfy his immediate
sexual desire and often can lead to a relationship of sorts. If a
woman isn't aware of the different intentions behind a man's
itemizing behavior, it can cause a misunderstanding or
miscommunication the confusion comes into play when it
means one thing to him and she takes his interest to mean
something else. Chocolate is notorious for itemizing his prey.

Itemizing isn't exclusive to men, women itemize men as well.
The difference is when a woman sees a man with a great chest
or big biceps and finds that she is very attracted to him based
on his physique, seldom does she go with her sexual
impulses. She often thinks about the big picture and questions
the circumstances: Is this a man I can trust? Do we have other
compatibilities? Will he find me as attractive? Being such an
attractive man, can he be loyal or is he a player? The hopeless
romantics or the women that don't look beyond a man's biceps
and big hands are naïve, or they are only seeking physical,
short term pleasure. By contrast, men habitually only see the

small picture and the immediate gratification of sex. Rarely do they consider the cause and effect of their actions with women or the big picture. It isn't until after the fact (sex that is) that a man sees the bigger picture, in which case, only because he is forced to.

On any given afternoon Jake sees a great pair of legs on a slender built 5'7" blonde. Her face and the rest of her body are attractive, but it is her legs that fascinate him. Focusing only on her legs, he can immediately begin to fantasize about her in a sexual manner. His imagination can run wild. Even in that fledging moment he thinks of strategies to meet her, see more of her or to sleep with her if he feels that is a viable option; all done with as little effort as possible.

What doesn't run through his mind is "I can't wait to spend money on her, wouldn't those legs look great in a pair of Jimmy Choos." Nor is he feeling the need to have sex with her because there is an emotional connection or he thinks they have a potential future together. He may imagine her as his girlfriend, but at that moment it's his animal instinct at work, the hunt if you will. The conquest of having that woman with the great pair of legs, in his bed, her bed, the back of his car, or in a lonely motel, wherever it can happen; he just wants her. Again, he is not thinking about the big picture.

Men can't help but initially see you as a body part. It's just the way men are built and they've been that way for centuries. This is especially true when you meet for the first time at a bar, night club, party, walking down the street, or even in a grocery store. Don't be offended, be flattered. Some of you are disagreeing and think you shouldn't be flattered and I'm a jerk for saying that you should be. You see yourself as more than a great pair of legs and want to be seen as such. I couldn't agree with you more. The truth is your physical beauty doesn't say anything about your intelligence, your ability to love unconditionally, or your caring heart. The physical you is his first impression. Attracting the opposite sex is flattering.

What if the relationship develops into something serious? Wouldn't you love the fact that your man finds you intellectually and physically attractive? In all fairness, you only judge a man on what you see physically. Besides, I've never known a woman who doesn't want to be admired for her beauty, even if only for her luscious lips or her great legs.

A man sees a woman as a whole person if there is time to get to know her, such as a work environment, social circle, or any surroundings where he has the adequate time to get to know her better. Time is on a woman's side when getting to know a man. Has it ever happened that a man confesses that he thought you were one way, but now sees you as another?

This doesn't mean he isn't attracted to her breasts or that his goal to sleep with her has diminished. His desires are still there, except that he sees more of her personality and consequentially has to see the bigger picture. Every day when her great pair of legs walks past his desk he will think twice whether or not to have a one night stand with her fearing the repercussions if things don't work out, i.e. losing his job or a sexual harassment lawsuit. If you are part of a social group, he knows he has a social responsibility to the group and sleeping with different women in the group is a no no. To remain in the group he has to abide by the non-verbal rules. There are always exceptions to the rule. There are men who will never care to see the big picture. They are selfish and self-centered.

Once a woman dresses provocatively she is more than likely accentuating one or more of her best physical assets with the intention of attracting a male. Without a doubt she understands that men do itemize. When she dresses sexy she in fact setting up the bull's-eye so there is no mistaking what her best assets are. Her skirt is a little higher to show off her legs and her top lower to show off her breasts. There is nothing wrong with dressing and feeling sexy. Men love it and it works like a charm.

When a sexy woman gets together with a man without thinking about the big picture and if she doesn't ask the right questions, she can find herself greatly disappointed in the end. No woman is going to pretend that her sexy outfit is to prove how smart she is and how much love she has in her heart. No man can read a woman's mind and it's never obvious to a man what she isn't communicating verbally. He will pursue her for what it's worth and nothing more: sexy girl - sexy outfit - horny man - physical attraction - consenting adults. If she wanted something more or wanted to be seen for her inner beauty, she will be disappointed wearing a skimpy dress.

More common than not, once the sexual act is done he could very easily regret the experience and realize that he isn't that attracted to her after all. Men can't make rational decisions about how they feel about a woman until after sex. That might sound shallow, but it's true. He might become distant and withdrawn emotionally. I'm sure most of you experienced being with a guy and him not calling the next day. You say to yourself what's up with that? What's wrong with me? What did I do wrong? This can be especially confusing and frustrating because most likely the man flattered you to bring you closer prior to sleeping with you. Then after sex he behaves the complete opposite.

True story — Bunny and Scott meet online through a dating service on a Monday afternoon. Scott sees her photograph and is very attracted to her and her double D breasts. Tuesday they go on a date. Nothing too special, they meet at a coffee shop and talk about themselves and how much they are attracted to one another. On their date Scott confirms Bunny's breast size, something the online photograph couldn't do, which only made Scott desire her more. At the end of the date they kiss good night. Later that night and throughout the week they stay in touch via email. The more they connect the more intimate and personal the conversation becomes. By Thursday they talk about moving to a different city together. Scott said to Bunny that she is his dream girl. By now its four days later and they feel they trust each other well enough to consummate the relationship. Friday night Scott spends the night at Bunny's house. This would also be their second date and the second time they actually see each other in person. Bunny is excited because for the past five days Scott has said things that are music to her ears. On Friday, they meet at Bunny's house. After some light conversation and a tour of her house, they immediately head to the bedroom where they have sex – twice.

By midnight these two souls were satisfied and pretty tired. Just as they are about to call it a night, Scott tells Bunny they need to talk. Bunny anticipated hearing more music to her ears. Instead he admits that they can only be friends. He thought he wanted to be in a relationship with her and move to a new city together, but he realizes that his career is more important. Bunny is shocked and a bit broken hearted to say the least.

Prior to sleeping together, Scott said everything he thought Bunny wanted to hear to bring her closer to him. He didn't say what she wanted because he knew and cared about her, he doesn't even know her. All he really wanted was the conquest - in this case it is her double D breasts. Also, Scott really couldn't make a rational decision on how he felt until after they had sex. Once the deed is done, he could think clearly and see the whole picture. Had Scott been able to see the whole picture clearer prior to sleeping together, he probably would have passed on the opportunity to be with Bunny.

Scott should have never encouraged the conversation about moving to a new city together in the first week or mentioned that Bunny is his dream woman. He knew she wasn't his dream girl and he had no intention of leaving the city. This is what men do and this is how men think. Men have and will say anything when they are itemizing to win the prize. On the other hand, Bunny should have been smart enough to know better; after all she is in her thirties.

After Scott dropped the bomb on Bunny, she confronted him on the mixed messages he was sending her. Tongue tied, Scott is speechless. He might have been lost for words, but his eyes saw the consequences of his actions. Bunny attempts to recoup some of Scott's sentimental words from earlier in the week, but her voice messages fall on deaf ears. Scott doesn't feel a strong need to give her what she needs and desires. After sex, Scott sees the bigger picture and makes his evaluation that they should be friends. Although she has great double D breasts, which he loves and is very attracted to, he now looks at her other qualities and assets. Whatever traits Scott needs to call a woman his dream girl, Bunny is lacking them. Her legs are not so perfect, her smile and laugh are not to his liking. Scott now can only see Bunny as no more than a convenient sex partner. He actually says to Bunny that they can be friends with benefits. In defeat, she agrees.

If you are a woman who only wants to be the friend with benefits, fantastic it's a win - win arrangement. If on the other hand, you use your sexy outfit as a lure to get his attention or you sleep with him with the hidden agenda that he'll be your man, it can backfire. If you think you can handle just a physical relationship, but you discover you are now emotionally attached, it's too late. The reason being is that once a man sees you as a friend with benefits, a booty call, or a one-night stand it's very hard for him to make the connection that you are commitment / girlfriend material. It's not fair, but it is true. Scott will never see Bunny as his woman.

We all know how difficult it is for a woman to be lovers with to a guy she has declared as a friend. Once a guy is in the friend zone with a female, no matter what the guy does, he can send flowers, gifts, take her to fancy dinners, and even remember her mother's birthday, but she just can't make the transition from friend to lover. The same is true for men. Once a relationship based on a body part is established, it is possible that will never change to something more. Although many couples have attempted to prove otherwise, they generally fail at being more. There is a saying amongst men that, "A whore can never be a housewife." I'm not calling anyone a whore or trying to hurt anyone's feelings, I am only telling the truth.

The frustration and confusion in thousands of relationships is that they began on physical attraction, one physical attribute without boundaries, rules, terms, or conditions. As a result, the relationship meanders in no particular direction and the rules are set by non-communication. Without directions, a woman's needs are not going to be met. She will need and want more direction, but too often she is afraid to ask. She needs to ask constructive questions of herself, of him, and of the relationship. Without constructive question they are headed for disappointment, just as Mimi allows Jake to do as he pleases.

A woman wears a sexy outfit that lures a man to her. In return, he says all the right things, "Baby you are so sexy, I can't wait to kiss you and spend my every waking hour with you." The next thing you know, the two strangers are in bed under the sheets, no direction, no terms and no conditions. This frequent scenario reminds me of a song by Morris Day and the Time - "*If the Kid Can't Make You Come*" from their Ice Cream Castle album. In the song, Morris is having sex with a woman who he recently met. They are getting it on and everything is great until she asks him, "Morris, what is my name?" He pauses and replies, "Baby... ain't it?" She thought she could handle the one-night stand without getting to know him better, but she realizes she needs to ask some of the bigger questions. She knows he has itemized her and is only interested in the conquest. Because men don't think about the big picture and the consequences, Morris answers with **Baby ain't it**, versus being responsive to her changed feelings and taking the time to get to know the woman who is in his bed.

After itemizing and sex, the man is physically satisfied and the woman is emotionally and quite possibly, physically dissatisfied. In most cases the woman doesn't climax. She is more interested in having connection. She believes she is with a man that is more interested in her than sex and that the encounter of intimacy will lead to more than a one-night stand. What she wants he can't give, because for him it is convenience sex that went too far. It's not supposed to be a relationship.

Unfortunately, men are too cautious to be honest. In the beginning, they should lay it on the line and say exactly what they want, but they fear hurting her feelings. Then they wait too long to be honest, fearing they will be cut off from sex in retaliation. He can no longer ignore the bigger picture and feels stuck – the divide between staying in the relationship and being dishonest and unfulfilled or having integrity and leaving. As a substitute for honesty, he pretends as long as he is getting what he wants and she keeps hoping that he will change and give her more of his time not just the late night kind. The best he can do is to pray the relationship will end due to extenuating circumstances.

To avoid empty sex based on your chocolate desiring your specific body part, make it *your* responsibility that he gets to know who you are. It's not his responsibility to figure out your great qualities. Don't rely on the classic verbiage, *if he really cares about me he would find out who I really am. If he really cares, he would know how I feel and what I need. If he really cared, it would be obvious.* Where is it written that men are mind readers? Think of it as a job interview. No matter what you wear or what your resume says, you do your best to sell the employer on your skills, your talents, integrity, honesty, loyalty, commitment, and so on. No one sits in an interview thinking "If this human resources employee really wants me to work here, they would figure out how great I am." With that attitude you would never get a job. How is it possible for the human resources department to see you as a neat organized professional, if your resume has typos, misspelled words, and incomplete information? If a woman dresses provocatively on a date, how can she expect a man to see her as a woman he wants to bring home to his mother? You wouldn't go into a job interview unprepared. The same is true when dating chocolate, don't go unprepared.

Let him know who you are. Don't lie and pretend you are more or less than what you are. Be honest. I'm not saying give him your life history in detail. Nor am I saying share your wedding ideas with him. However, let him know that what he sees is what he gets. Better you tell him who you are now, than him finding out who you are not down the road. Be warned that men are not the best listeners, especially when sex is involved. Make sure he hears what you are saying. Engage in a conversation that forces him to see the big picture. By the way, your chocolate will love having these boundaries.

If you spend the time getting to know each other and you are a great listener, after three dates you'll know if he is sincere. You'll know if he likes you beyond your itemized body part. Sometimes your body part doesn't necessarily mean your bare legs or mini skirt. Discuss itemizing with him. Ask him what physically is most attractive about you. If you have a great pair of legs and he's attracted to you, then ask him what shape and size breasts turn him on or off. If he likes big breasts and yours are small have the conversation that you are a B cup and not D. He'll likely say that it's okay. Ask again and be sure it's really ok. It's almost like a cross examination. If he questions why you are asking, tell him that he's itemizing and that he sounds as though he'll sleep with a woman based on her breast size and not for whom she is and afterward he'll probably lose interest. That simple conversation will open up a lot of dialogue and you'll get to the bottom line. Its better the truth comes out now and not after you've had sex and he is nowhere to be found. Save some of the small talk for later. If things don't work out after the first date, it doesn't matter that his home town is Rockford, Illinois or that he loves horses. You'll both be going your separate ways. You don't want to overwhelm him, but you want to get to the nuts and bolts of what is going on between you both.

Being sexy and accentuating the best of the physical you is great because it does lure men to you. Once they are lured in, you can choose. Don't be delusional and needy to a point that you don't want to hear the truth. Don't pretend that he loves you or your breasts when he doesn't. Pretending something is there when it's not will get results you do not desire. Once you are a booty call, friend with benefits, or a one-night stand, that's the category you'll stay in. I am generalizing, and yes, there are exceptions to the rule. Don't hedge your bet that you or your Jake is the exception. Approach him with all the generalities.

Ninety-nine percent of rejections you get from a man the morning after will come from him not seeing the big picture and instead seeing you as a particular body part. It's certainly not because he connected to your inner beauty or book smarts.

When men itemize it makes them more attracted to a larger pool of women, than if he sees them as the whole package. Jake sees a great pair of legs, sexy breasts, or a beautiful face that he is attracted to a minimum of three times on any given day. He is attracted enough to have sex with her based on her best asset. Three times nine equals twenty-seven body parts per day times 365 equals 9855 women a year a man is attracted to or desires to be with based on one body part or another. This doesn't include the women on Myspace, Facebook, or Craigslist. If he could see women as a whole he would only be attracted to 10% or less of all the women he sees.

Don't confuse an itemized desire as a whole package deal or that it will equal a long-term relationship. Women, instead of accentuating a specific body part or two to get men's attention, why not accentuate the whole you. Show some breast and brains. I know that it is easier to accent your breast than your brain (I'm not being derogatory), but most women especially the attractive ones won't do the self-help to make themselves more attractive to most men beyond the outer beauty. One way to be more attractive to a man is not to let the relationship be all about you or your neediness. Being too needy is bad for everyone. Neediness makes your partner responsible for you emotionally. No one wants to be responsible for another person's emotions. It's hard enough being responsible for our own emotional needs. Live in self-worthiness. Avoid asking those insecure questions such as, "Do I look fat in these jeans?" "Now that we kissed or had sex what does this mean?" "Will you call me?" And one of the biggest no no of all, is asking a man in one form or another the question, "What does it mean?"

One of the biggest turn off's has to be a lack of confidence. Confidence is always attractive regardless of gender. When a woman lacks confidence and is needy she relies on the sure thing, which is her body, and a man proceeds to itemize her. When a man sees the whole woman and they enter into a relationship, he won't be disappointed physically and emotionally after the initial thrill is gone because he sees her for whom she is. When he sees the whole picture it will be easier for you to close the deal. When approached by a suitor, you will be able to decipher his intentions. Males are so programmed to itemize, they can't always distinguish the difference between their genuine curiosities about you as a woman or itemizing body parts.

Emotional Itemization

Emotional itemization is another way men itemize women. He meets a woman or has known a woman for a while. Not looking at the big picture of who she is, he is attracted to her for one reason or another. It certainly is not because he has taken the time to get to know her. Being paranoid and expecting rejection from women in general, Tom doesn't make a move or let it be known he is attracted to her. These suppressed feelings of attraction can linger on for days or even years. Then one day the woman Tom has been harboring feelings for gives him a warm compliment, does a kind gesture or gives him an invitation, after all they are platonic friends. Whatever her gesture, at that very moment he takes her attentiveness as an opportunity to pursue her. Tom feels validation and acceptance, which triggers feelings in him that she is interested or open to a possibility – maybe just maybe he has a shot. She lends her kindness to him because she sees him as a harmless threat.

He reads her one flattering remark as a sign that she is interested. When in reality she is being a nice person, with no other intentions. From a woman's simple goodwill gesture, men can create ideas about a potential relationship with her. He can hold onto these feelings for you even while he is in a committed relationship. Tom isn't looking at the whole picture, he is simply itemizing her based on emotions the same way Scott itemized Bunny physically. If you've experienced a guy like Tom, you've learned to keep your guard up and rarely throw random compliments.

Women definitely recognize that men do emotionally itemize them from the slightest gesture to a platonic invitation. Once he receives the welcomed attention from her, he frequently needs and will want more. It feels good to him. His neediness can become a thorn in her side as he'll repeat his previous behavior hoping she will repeat her kind gesture. For example, a guy name Doug, mid-forties, married with children, had a tutor come to his home to help his eldest daughter with her math skills. The tutor happened to be an attractive twenty-year-old, who was smart, but a little inexperienced in relationships with men. Being naïve and honest, she tells the father that she really liked the shirt he is wearing and how handsome he looked. She said it with the intention that the father wouldn't take it as anything more than a passing compliment. The father thanked her and she went back to tutoring. The following week when she arrived to tutor the kids, the father is wearing the same shirt and looking for her validation. He continues to wear that shirt several weeks in a row. The tutor recognized that her compliment actually made him interested in her. As a matter of protection and to cease it from going farther, she acted a little bitchy toward him. The tutor never again said a word about his wardrobe or gave any other compliment for that matter. I'm sure she learned a lot about men and how they itemize emotionally.

Mint Chocolate ~

"Simply put... everyone has a price, mine is chocolate!"
Anonymous

Closing the Deal

You meet your chocolate, that's tall dark and handsome. He spends quality time with you and makes your heart go *coo coo for coco pops*. Things couldn't be better; the only thing missing is his commitment. Now that he's got you, how do you get him to close the deal? Maybe you want him to think of you as his one and only or you want him to ask you to marry him. In any event, how do you get him to commit or take the relationship to the next level?

Can you get him to marry you without having a hidden agenda, e.g., intentionally getting pregnant, or using threats or ultimatums: "If you don't marry me by such and such a date the relationship is over?"... Or without badgering him with, "Are you afraid of commitment?" "What are you waiting for, my clock is ticking? If you really care about me then you would marry me?" "My girlfriend got married after dating her boyfriend for only one year." The answer is yes you can. This is Mimi's challenge. She ultimately wanted Jake to ask her to marry him or at the very least wanted a long-term committed relationship.

Although these methods do get men to marry women, wouldn't it be better and wouldn't you feel better if you learned how to manage your chocolate and get him to ask you of his own free will? Wouldn't Mimi feel better about herself if Jake thought that highly of her? Wouldn't Mimi want to share her joy with her family and friends that of all the women in the world Jake honored her that highly and, more importantly, he did it without being coerced? Wouldn't that feel more authentic? I think we all would agree the answer is yes. Being pressured or manipulated resonates with resentful feelings. When you force someone to do something under duress, you'll always have doubt about their commitment.

Before Mimi can close the deal with Jake, she needs to understand some of the ironies of attractions vs. marriage between the sexes. She also needs to learn a few more fundamentals about the Jakes and some honesty about herself as a woman.

Jake is like all men. He too has a strong need for a women's attention. Reminiscent of the need for validation by his mother combined with the rejection men receive on a daily basis, makes him easy chocolate prey for you. It doesn't take much work for a woman to grab a man's attention. As all women know, a simple smile or a glance is enough to get noticed by men. Once the man has bitten her bait, the guy is vulnerable and will do the necessary steps to receive more of her attention, provided she wants it.

To take her allure one step further, a man is even more vulnerable if the woman dresses and behaves provocatively in his presence. He becomes lustful and submissive putty in her hands. To capitalize on the opportunity, he will spend his hard earned money on dinners, travel, gifts, and lots of sweet talk to be with her, all for her validation and sex. To further illustrate the importance and power of a women's allure, at any given time he will neglect or push aside some of his personal and business affairs to spend quality time with her and give her excessive attention - all to win her affection.

Once trapped in her allure, he is only thinking of ways to please this woman. Ironically, all of these deeds are sometimes before they ever have sex, (i.e. Tom Cruise and Katie Holmes as of June 2005, according to the celebrity entertainment magazines).

A mega movie star, Tom Cruise caught the glance of a younger attractive woman whom he proposed to after six weeks of dating. As it is the same for most women, Katie did little work to get his attention. Maybe a smile or a hello really is all it took to get Tom hooked. She didn't have to wine and dine him or take him on an expensive trip. I'm not saying Katie didn't do anything, but Tom did the majority of the work to move their relationship forward. I can assure you, Tom, as busy as he is, cut some events out of his daily routine to spend quality time with her. I know some of you are thinking men are supposed to do all the work because they are men. The point I'm making is that it took very little effort from Katie. By contrast it took Tom a heap of effort.

Taking it even one step further, for a woman to get a man to have sex with her is just as easy as to get him to turn his head, if not easier. If any woman were to suggest to a man that she would like some physical pleasure, most guys would jump at the opportunity. How many guys would turn down available sex? Not many. Granted it might not be your dream guy, the safest, the most enjoyable or a long lasting relationship, but women can get sex any night of the week.

So the question remains, how is it possible for a woman to almost effortlessly get a man's attention, have sex with a man with ease, but almost impossible for a woman, at least from her point of view, to get a man to commit to a relationship? How does a woman get her man to ask for her hand in marriage on his own? It seems quite ironic. Is it just the way men are? Do men just prefer to be single? Are men by nature commitment phobic? Or…Are there definitive reasons?

Because men naturally want to sow their oats everywhere, there is really one way to have him focus on one woman and that is in his mind she has to be the one and only. She has to be the better deal – the only deal in town. He needs to feel it doesn't get any better than her. When he is confronted by the allure of another woman, he needs to think to himself, "I have my queen; I'm not interested in any other woman." He'll also feel that he doesn't want any other man with his woman. He will want to marry her so that she isn't available, taking her off the dating market.

A man wants to invest in the relationship. Men are logical. They invest for a return. The more they invest, the deeper their commitment. No investment, no commitment. Your good looks alone won't close the deal, they will entice him. Men don't invest in sex or good looks; he'll investment in potential and possibility. What makes it special for men is how he feels about the woman; Sex with a hooker – low investment – very little meaning; sex with a loving, sexy, intelligent, funny, low drama, loving and nurturing girlfriend – high investment – greater meaning. Although sex alone won't close the deal because logically for a man sex is just that, sex, and looks fade over time. In the big picture sex is a need for men not a want.

Don't confuse what happens in the beginning of your relationship as a long-term investment for him. It is a short-term investment with little gain. After you've been together for a while and the newness of each other wears off that is when the long-term investment accountability begins.

His investment is to make you the best mate for him and in exchange he will provide for you and be the best boyfriend, husband and / or father that he can be. The best example is found in the relationship between your grandparents. Their relationship is most likely based on grandpa working and grandma being a stay-at-home wife. Grandpa is fully invested in grandma because she knows exactly what, when, and how grandpa likes things. This is not to say that grandpa doesn't care about grandma's needs and wants. I'll bet he knows her dos and don'ts quite well. Besides this is about closing the deal, like grandma did forty years ago to win grandpa over. Ask married elders what their secrets are for a long term or happy marriage. The one thing you probably won't hear the woman saying is "Be independent. Be selfish and forget his needs and if he is particular – screw him."

Through her actions, he tests the potential of his investment when he asks his woman to prepare his breakfast, lunch, and dinner a certain way. He'll tell her how cold he likes his beer or how many meatballs he wants in his spaghetti. He'll teach or tell her how he wants to be pleased sexually. Also he will tell her how he prefers you to dress or what perfume is his favorite. He'll evaluate how you handle yourself in public. Every man has his own criteria on what he looks for in his investment, even men who can't articulate what they are looking for. If he is the quiet type, take charge and ask him what he wants.

You'll enter your relationship with an upper hand. He'll think you must be heaven sent. Indifferent women will argue and resist her man's investment criteria – she'll say, "He is so picky – why should I do that for him – what's in it for me – I'm tired – it's not all about him, he is selfish" These women aren't very smart, especially if this is a man they really would like to be with. Granted some men are pushovers and accept the bantering as par for the course, but a strong man will see that commentary as annoying. He is less likely to see you as marriage material. The weak man can be manipulated into marriage, but you want your man strong and for him to ask for your hand in marriage.

A secret about men is that when they see their women as great, in his eyes it's very difficult for him to imagine another man getting all the perks that she is providing for him. He doesn't want to imagine you cooking for another man or giving another man your unconditional sex and love. When his needs are met: he is receiving great sex, great love, dinner, support, attention, understanding, room to watch sports, see his buddies, and not be nagged, etc. - you better believe he is ready to take you off the singles market. He'll also be the first to step up and say to another man, "Hey that's my lady... hands off buddy." Now he is protecting his investment. The more his needs are met the deeper the investment, the more he will protect his investment. The greater the investment, the greater the chances are for him to ask for your hand in marriage. If his needs are not being met, he'll care less whether you are with another guy, hanging out at a club, and certainly will not care for marriage.

It's a woman's responsibility to ask her man specifically what's most important for him in his investment. Find out what his favorite meals are, movie genres, beverages, his favorite sports, and how, when and where he wants sex. Ask him directly. Don't read his mind or expect him to read yours. Direct communication is the key. Men love to hear how much, why, when, how, where, and what. You'll have fun getting to know each other and asking those types of questions will keep you both connected.

Another important secret about men is that they love to brag about their woman to their friends. Most guys are complaining about what their woman won't do or has not done. When you give your man what he desires and satisfy his needs, believe me he'll brag about you to all his friends. They will be your greatest ally. Guys know how hard it is to get a great girl. When they see their friend with a great woman, they'll encourage him to marry her. They'll say she's a keeper or you better marry her before you lose her. You want his friends to think of you that way, vs. "Dude your girl is a bitch."

Among men, it's a special thing for one man to tell another man to get married. When a fellow friend doesn't necessarily agree with his choice, he will say something or remain neutral. You want his friends to promote the idea of him getting married or deepen his commitment. That is the highest compliment a man can give or receive. It's easy to brag about how gorgeous his bride might be, but every man wants to get back into the womb, so meet his needs.

When he boasts about his girl, every guy listening envies him because at the end of the day that's what all men want. Years ago I dated a very nurturing woman who loved to cook and take care of her man. By the way, I love those types of women – yes, of course; they remind me of my mother. Anyhow, she is a really great cook and the type of person who would give you the shirt off her back. While sitting around at work talking to some of the guys about my relationship, I'll never forget this one guy who is a famous actor and famous for being with the ladies. He said to me, "Really your girl cooks and cleans for you? I wish my girls would do that for me. All the girls I date complain that I'm not doing enough." He went on to say, "I need to get my girl to understand that's what I need – I want to be taken care of." Generally speaking, women approach relationships with a "What's in it for me" attitude. I believe the "What's in it for me" attitude comes from fear, insecurity, and issues from a previous relationship. I think that anyone that enters a relationship should ask the question. How can I contribute? How can I help?

Motivation

What is a man's motivation to be in a committed relationship?

1. He wants attention in the form of validation and admiration.

2. He wants to be taken care of.

3. Sex and plenty of it.

4. Freedom to be a guy and do what guys do, i.e. watch sports, and hang with the guys.

5. Take interest and indulge him in his career. Also, keep yourself interesting, get a hobby.

6. Don't be needy – needing a lot of attention. You are an adult, not a six-year-old.

7. Don't give to get. Give unconditionally.

8. Respect – if he has earned it.

9. Pick up where his mother left off. Follow her blueprint.

10. He doesn't want to come home to another challenge.

When a man comes home from work, the last thing he wants to do when he walks through the door is fight. If you are a working girl you know that you spend eight hours fighting, being challenged by your occupation, co-workers and traffic. When you come home you want peace, love, connection, and support. I'm certain many of you are saying to yourself, "I do take an interest in all of the above, but he still doesn't want to commit." If a man doesn't want to be married, and is choosing to be single for the rest of his life, there is nothing you or I can do.

When you are winning a man over, you have to do it from the value and position of how can I give, how can I help? Not – what's in it for me. The "What about me?" and "What's in it for me?" syndrome is a subtle turn off for men. They don't brag about how needy his woman is. The reason I say subtle is because men are so used to hearing women, in one form or another say, "What about me?" Men take it as a par for the course. That doesn't mean they like it and certainly they are not turned on by it. The "Me Syndrome" is really apparent when you watch the *ABC* television show "*The Bachelor*." The show takes place over a ten-week period, beginning with twenty-five women to choose from and each week he eliminates a contestant down to his final choice. If you can watch the show without getting emotionally involved and pay attention to what the women are saying, you'll understand what I mean by the "Me Syndrome." As I watch the show, I listen to what each bachelorette says to convince the bachelor to pick her. Rarely, if ever, do they have conversations that begin with the phase "What can I do... to make your life better?" "What can I do to make your career better?" or "What can I do to be the best partner for you? If any of the women said that, the bachelor would see it as a potential relationship to invest in. They rarely ask the right questions because they are looking at the opportunity for their own gain. They want to know, "What am I going to get out of it." One bachelorette said she needed to get married soon because her eggs were rotting. What do her eggs have to do with his needs? The other conversations you hear are how they feel a strong connection. Feeling a strong connection is about "Me." When men hear "What's in it for me," they feel a sense of responsibility that they aren't necessarily ready to hear or emotionally ready to deal with. Imagine if he dated a woman who said my eggs are rotting and I need a baby. He would feel under constant pressure, which doesn't sound very attractive. Versus, a woman who says to her man, "How can I contribute to the success of your career?" How can I help?

The winning approach is to ask him empowering questions, such as, "How do you like your coffee in the morning? How do you like your women to dress?" The number one question that should be asked is – "Which way do you feel most loved?" Then be willing to fulfill that need. The question is so powerful that it immediately compels him to invest in you. Mimi thought that by doing things for Jake that he had an invested interest in her, he didn't. She only saw it from her point of view of what's in it for me. She never asked Jake which way he felt most loved. His investment in her is superficial. When you approach from a point of view of "How can I help," the investment stakes are raised and hence a deeper connection is created. Remember, no long-term investment – no commitment.

Interesting point – All over the world, the relationship between mothers and their children is always – How can I help? How can I make your life better? Mothers don't have children and say, what's in it for me? What about me? Granted that some parents do have the attitude, "What about me?", but generally speaking parents especially mothers want to help and want to give. Remember men's first and most important influence is his relationship with his mother. Mothers are instinctually smart enough to know that in giving to her child, she receives without asking. By contrast, women are often afraid to give for fear they won't receive. Or...They measure how much they give and expect the same amount in return. An excellent example of this is if the size of the ring equals the love in his heart... "If you really care you would..."

You could argue that a mother can love her child unconditionally because they'll always be there, a man could leave. However, men have a natural impulse to give to a woman. In all of men's accomplishments, somewhere in the equation it equates to pleasing a woman. Whether it's building a tall skyscraper, owning an airline, erecting a monument, an athletic achievement, or becoming a manager of a fast food chain restaurant, a woman is in his consideration. It could be in the form of affording dinner, buying her gifts, or having dinner on his beachfront property. Men want to please a woman. Sexually, a mature man will do his best to please the woman first, then himself. Fear not – you'll have your needs met. Men want to please their woman. When men's needs are met, they are very willing to meet your needs. This is not to say that you have to meet his needs first to have your needs met. This chapter is on closing the deal, not equality. Men are simple and need very little to be happy. The less complicated their lives are, the better. If a man can watch sports, have sex, play with his gadgets, or hang out with friends every now and then, he's happy. Men rarely care about the details of things, such as the color of the new drapes or whether or not your hair is layered or cut blunt.

From the time a boy is old enough to beg his mother, he is learning to close the deal. If you have a brother or you have a son, you've witnessed him pleading for something he wants from his mother. He doesn't stop until she says yes. I'm sure some of you have experienced being with a man that wanted to have sex with you so bad that he begged and gave you every reason why you should take your clothes off. Eventually you gave in.

To close the deal, enter the relationship with the attitude, of what can I give and how can I help. A man wants to invest in his partner. Make your value as a woman as high as possible so that he has no other choice, but to want to be committed to you...always and forever.

Chocolate Fudge ~

*"To the ancient Mayans it is the nectar of the gods.
Europeans revered it as a symbol of wealth and power.
African cultures believed it was an aphrodisiac. One of the
world's greatest expressions of taste and rapture, chocolate is
enjoyed by millions..."* Lake Champlain Chocolates

The Review
Milk Chocolate ~ The Chocolate Relationship ~

You discovered the difference between salad and chocolate. You met Mimi and Jake and read the mistakes they made as a couple and individually. They lacked communication and lacked boundaries. Mimi realized that she is addicted to chocolate, but never knew how to manage it. Addiction - *the state of being enslaved to a habit or practice of something that is psychologically or physically habit-forming.* She also learned that listening to her friends and family's advice regarding the dangers of chocolate isn't necessarily the best advice, especially the suggestion that she should conform to be with Bob. For Mimi, a mixed-green salad will never do. Chocolate will always prevail over salad and isn't this true about dieting? With all the healthy food that is good for you, you'll always lust after your favorite dessert Chocolate.

Chocolate Truffle ~ We Like What We Like ~

Don't feel guilty or be persuaded from your desires and wants, excluding, of course, life threatening situations. You, me and the whole world likes what we like. The last thing we want is someone to tell us not to be happy or how we should be happy. The key is to learn to manage your desires, be it sweets, coffee, sodas, food, or you're chocolate. Not knowing how to manage them could result in costly emotional and physical consequences.

White & Dark Chocolate ~ Why We Like Who We Like ~

Our childhood influences set the stage for our life values. The most influential and important relationship is with our parents. When the father is absent or emotionally unavailable, the daughter will grow up to desire chocolate. As a child, she has learned that love is something you compete for; therefore, she will be attracted to men who she needs to compete for to get attention. Generally speaking, these guys are not the accountants, lawyers, or schoolteachers. They tend to be the unemployed, unavailable artist, musician, actor, or surfer types. – Although, accountant and lawyer types do make great salads.

Chocolate Chip ~ Filling In The Gap ~

The first thirty days or so of your new hot and passionate relationship you experience a major adrenaline rush. Both of you are competing with yourselves to get your once-perfect solid block of cheese, which is now Swiss, filled with all the emotions that were chipped away as a child. You crave and aspire to fill your gaps. The need is so strong that it can be addictive. Your new partner is your drug dealer of emotions and you can't wait to see him to so that you can get your fix. The addiction is the greatest high you'll ever have. As with any addict or addiction, you need your fix. You'll go to extreme measures to make sure that happens. You might literally beg for him to come back into your life. Remember the song *And I Am Telling You,* which the character Effie sang in the Broadway play and motion picture *"Dreamgirls?"* She is addicted to her man and demands that he stays and loves her. That's a love addiction. The high is so great to some that they'll continually bounce from relationship to relationship to stay within the thirty to forty-five day range. That is where the highest of high is for both partners. We all need our Swiss filled, but beware to what extreme you'll go to have it filled. The only permanent way to fill your cheese is to do the self-help work that is necessary. Over time and with new tools, you'll fill your Swiss cheese to resemble your once solid block of cheese.

White Chocolate ~ Setting Terms & Conditions ~

In all aspects of your life there are terms and conditions. If you breach the verbal or written contract, there are consequences. Be sure to have the values, reprimand, or penalties in place in your relationship. This is the right time and place "Not to settle." Anything less will have irreversible consequences. Get the rules straight from the very beginning. It will make your relationship flow that much easier and he'll have a higher level of respect for you.

Assorted Chocolate ~ Our Fundamental Needs ~

We all have six basic needs – the need for certainty, uncertainty, significance, connection, contribution, and growth. There are four basic ways we feel most loved: being held, being looked in the eyes, being shown, or being told. These triggers influence you into or out of a relationship. Know which way you feel most loved and which way your man feels most loved. Don't let myths such as love conquers all, there is "The One," a soul mate, or chemistry is all that matters misguide you in your relationships.

Solid Milk Chocolate ~ Defining a Relationship ~

We all want a solid long-lasting relationship. To start a relationship you have to be honest about yourself and your significant other. How much do you really know about him and him about you? Are you as honest as you demand him to be? Does he know about your sexual discretions? What about you're past party binges? Do you know all about his? Probably not! We conveniently leave out details that we believe will put the brakes on our relationship or it's our fear of being judged negatively. The truth of the matter is you really don't know your partner 100%. No one is going to tell you everything and you certainly are not going to expose 100% of yourself to him. You are indeed strangers who have met and chosen to get to know each other better over a given period of time. Don't fool yourself and then one day you are saying, "I can't believe he did that." "How could you do that to me?" You really never knew him. You only learn who another person is based on your interest and how it serves you. Get to know your partner as best you can by continually asking probing questions, not just questions that are in your best interest.

LOVE ~

As humans, we have an insatiable appetite to give love and to be loved. It is in our nature to give that which we have an abundance of. Love being our greatest natural resource, our well of love runs deep. It is only when we give our love profusely to our significant other that conflicting issues arise. You can and should love your fellow man, animals, and children with vigor. However, sadly due to the physical conditioning from our influences via parents, school, and the media, we are conditioned not to accept the abundance of love we desire to give.

Sugar Free Chocolate – Your Soul Mate! – We as a society are very attached to the idea of a soul mate. It is defined as a person you connect with on a spiritual level and in perfect harmony. The dating web site E-harmony.com promotes this idea to market their web site. Any couple that I've met that claims to be soul mates behaved similar to any other couple I've met. They argue and hold on to resentment, just as any other couple does. Furthermore, their sex life wasn't much different. I don't see any advantage to claiming to have found a soul mate, other than the romantic idea of it all. With a 50% divorce rate in America, I have to believe that the couples who claim to be soul mates are removed from that statistic. I believe if you learn more about yourself and your partner learn to communicate, set boundaries, and have terms and conditions, you are going to get along better and in effect feel as though you were made for each other.

Chocolate (Hershey's) Kiss ~ Mother/Son Effect ~

A mother's influence on her son's prospective of life is monumental. In principle, when you meet her son someday the work is already done. The mother has set all the necessary emotional triggers of what love is or is not for him. All you have to do is pick up where the mother has left off. Get to know his relationship between him and his mother. Ask him if his mother knows his favorite color? The answer is usually no. I believe when a parent doesn't know specific details about their child's likes and dislikes, such as their favorite color, movie, song, or their goals, it says a lot about the intimacy between the parent and the child. The answer usually is "No, my mother doesn't know my favorite color." This is a sign that he is more a Jake than a Bob; love him accordingly.

Chocolate Caramel ~ Why Men Itemize ~

All men itemize women's body parts. Don't be offended. It is just the way it is. Women's lips, legs or her breasts are enough for a man to take an interest in her. Until he has sex with you, he won't see the big picture. He can only rationalize his immediate want. After sex, he'll see the whole you. The risk is that once he sees the whole you, he might be less attracted to you. It is your responsibility for him to see who you really are from the time you meet, to the time you consummate the relationship.

Mint Chocolate ~ Closing the Deal ~

You want to close the deal, but not by begging, conniving, or giving deadlines. You want him to choose you as his bride because you are the best deal. It doesn't get any simpler than that. Ask him how you can help and not enter the relationship with a "What's in it for me" attitude. Be honest about who he really is, your relationship, and most importantly about yourself. Don't pretend there is more to your relationship if there really is not. In the end, all you are going to do is complain about what your man is not. You are not desperate, so don't behave desperately. There are plenty of men wanting and willing to get married. Lastly, your good looks and sex alone won't close the deal. They will entice him, but sex alone won't do it. Sex is a need for a man not want. What makes sex special for the man is how he feels about the woman. Obviously, booty calls and friends with benefits are just a release for a man versus having an amazing experience with the woman he loves. Contrary to popular belief, men also want to feel connected and loved. Remember, he wants back into the womb... put your guard down and let him in.

Semi Sweet Chocolate ~

Here are some rules to remind you of what to do and what not to do with chocolate.

The Rules

Rule #1 ~ Men Can't Make a Rational Decision Before Sex

Before sex, men are not thinking about the big picture. Their hormones are doing the talking for them. Being goal orientated, he has one task on his mind and that is to get laid, have sex, get some release or whatever you want to call it. Don't get mad at him for it, this is how all men behave. Quite honestly, his father and his father's father and his father's, father's, father all did the same thing. Once a guy has his release he can think clearly and evaluate the situation. Men make their decision about the relationship based on what happens before, during, and after sex.

If on your first date you are at his apartment and there are photos of him with other women, don't start asking a hundred questions, such as "Who is that?" or "Which one is your ex?" Being even a little jealous and insecure is not good pre-sex behavior. It really doesn't matter who is in the pictures. He's not your boyfriend. Well, at least not in his eyes. If during sex, you are insecure about your body and sexual techniques not good. If he wants to do something sexual that you are uncomfortable with and your reaction is, "That's gross," - not good. If you are uncomfortable, don't make a scene out of it, stay cool and say it's not my thing. After sex, you want to cuddle close and share pillow talk. It might not be a good idea unless he initiates it. It can come off as being too needy and insecure. If after sex, you suggest making him something to eat, turn the game on the television, or let him sleep, believe me you got his attention. This will actually turn him on. He'll think to himself this is the coolest girl ever, definitely a keeper. Most girls get needy after sex. Their neediness makes men feel responsible for her feelings and that's a turn off. Being confident goes a long way. Also, don't test him. You know what I'm talking about. After sex don't ask him to go shopping with you to see how much he cares or ask how great the sex was or wasn't. After sex, he can think clearly and he'll recap and evaluate the before, during, and after sexual experience. You can't expect a man to make a rational decision about your relationship until after sex. The less needy and insecure you seem the better.

Rule #2 ~ Every Guy You Meet Is Not "The One"

When you stop thinking in terms of the one / soul mate you will open yourself up to more opportunities and you won't seem so desperate. You'll get the – "I'm not going to settle" mentality out of your head. You get fixated on one guy and think that he is literally the one and only guy in the world. Just because he said hello and smiled doesn't make him the "The One." He just might be a nice guy or he might be a real nag once you get to know him. Stop looking at a man as someone you can't live without. Don't lie to yourself and justify why you need to be with him and only him. There are more males in this world than him.

Rule #3 ~ It's Not a Relationship Before Sex

As far men are concern, it is not a relationship before sex. Because you are spending time chatting extensively, you might believe you are in a relationship and that you are in an exclusive relationship. You may also think you are in a relationship simply because it feels like a relationship. Even if you have had a couple of dates, it doesn't necessarily mean you are in a committed relationship. Generally speaking, for a man it's not a relationship because you haven't had sex.

Rules #4 ~ Have Self-respect Boundary

Develop a boundary scale of self-respect from 1 to 10, with 10 being very respectful and 1 being little or no respect. If your man is the type to push the boundaries to 5 then he is still respectful, but if he pushes to 4 or under, he is showing less and less respect. He is also testing to see how much he can get away with before you snap. It doesn't matter where he thinks you should snap. It's only important that you know where you will snap and let him know it. You need to have your own definition of what you think is disrespectful to you.

Each woman's breaking point is different. In your definition, know when your guy has pushed it to level 4, at which point you have to put your foot down. Something Mimi didn't do. You have to do something not only for the sake of your relationship and letting him know he has gone too far, but for your self-respect. Respect yourself if you want him to respect you. Your man needs to know what your boundaries are in the relationship and how much BS you are willing to put up with.

If your boundaries are reasonable, he will be more than willing to live within them. If the boundaries are unclear, he will push until they are established or move on to another girl that will set some boundaries.

Rule #5 ~ Don't Ask What He Thinks of You

Questions such as, "What is your first impression of me?" "What do you think of the date so far?" are not good questions and only lead to uncomfortable conversation. It puts both of you on the spot. These are questions an insecure person would ask and it will make you seem weak. You are also giving the impression that you care too much about what he thinks of you and that you are second-guessing yourself.

Being strong and confident makes a positive impression. One of men's biggest turn-on's a women's confidence. When he asks you what you think about him, tell him you think he's okay. It sounds mean, but he will love it. Don't ask what he thinks of you. The most important question is what you think of yourself. What you think of yourself is what you will project; your projection will be his opinion of you.

Rule #6 ~ Don't Ask What Does it Mean or Why Do You Say That?

These two have to be the biggest turn off questions for men. To a man's ear they are also trick questions, which men often hesitate to answer. His answer can turn her on or off. It's like being asked, "Do I look fat in these Blue jeans?"

When a man says to a woman, "You are the best lover" and she follows with, "What does that mean?" A guy will re-think the statement and her question to be certain he said the right thing. The majority of the time, when a man says I had a good time – it simply means he had a good time, nothing more nothing less. When a woman asks those questions, what she really wants to know is where she stands in the relationship. It's a back door way of seeking an answer to her insecurities. Through the trials and tribulations of screwing up their response in the past, men learn to think twice about their answers to these questions. The questions are unfair because they are loaded questions. If you want to know where you stand in the relationship, just ask, or observe what's going on in the relationship. If his phone is ringing off the hook at 2AM, it's probably another woman or a drug deal. What does it mean? It means he is seeing another woman. Where do you stand in the relationship? If you are married, he is probably not happy sexually in the relationship. Be honest; if you are married do you have a great sex life or not? Is he sexually satisfied? You know the answer.

Don't ask the trick questions to trick him for your own agenda. More importantly don't ask the question because you need to be confident and when you say, "What does that mean?" you sound surprised like "Wow, really, are you kidding me, I can't believe it." When you are at work and your boss says, "Great job. Sales are up this month. Thank you." You don't say – "What does that mean? Or "Why did you say that?" At work, you know you gave 100%; therefore, you understand the praise. Be that confident in your relationship. Be the best you can be. At the end of the day, he either gets you or he doesn't. When he said you are a great lover or that you are beautiful and smart, just reply with thank you. Look at him in the eyes and say, "Did you expect anything else?

Rule #7 ~ Don't Ask Him What Is His "Ideal" Woman

Don't ask what is his ideal woman, it's probably not you. His ideal woman has the lips of Angelina Jolie, the body of Halle Berry, the face of Lindsey Lohan, and the singing voice of Mariah Carey. You get the point? Don't set yourself up for rejection by asking this unnecessary question. You'll be left feeling as though you'll never be able to live up to his expectations. You don't need to ask what is his ideal woman is. Play your cards right and you are his ideal woman.

Rule #8 ~ Don't Kiss or Have Sex On The First Date

Don't feel you need to kiss or have sex on the first date. Kiss him on date three or four, especially if he is very attractive because the more attractive he is, the less enthusiastic you should be about kissing on the first date. Is there a difference between date one and date three or four in that you have to kiss or have sex on the first date? You waited all of your life to kiss this guy, so one or two dates won't make a difference. Even if it is the most awesome date, do not kiss him. Besides, he'll be more intrigued and wonder what to do next to make you want to kiss him. Be indifferent about it and call it a night. If he asks you to kiss him, tell him you aren't sure if you desire him yet.

My rule is: Kiss only as a prelude to passion.

Rule #9 ~ Treat Him the Way He Is Used To Being Treated

If your chocolate's past relationship was with an abusive woman, verbally or physically, (a bitch if you will) treat him as badly as he was treated or end the relationship with him before it begins. Better yet, treat him in the same manner as his mother. The bark sounds worst than the bite. You are not the Red Cross; you don't need to save him. Also don't take responsibility for the way he is raised. If he is a **level 2**, you can't make him a **level 1**. Giving him more than he thinks he deserves will lead him to say, "Bye, bye. You are the weakest link." If you can't handle that, then exit the relationship before it begins.

Rule #10 ~ Don't Like Him Too Much

Don't like him too much. Unfortunately, most of us aren't comfortable being cherished and placed on a pedestal; we prefer the chase. Before you get *coo coo for coco puffs* over chocolate, be sure you have emotional leverage - meaning he likes you more than you like him. The moment you like him more than you like yourself is the moment the relationship is to your disadvantage: black box - white box. Now your guy, who once cuddled up with you, needs space. Another common excuse he gives you is that he isn't happy and that something is missing. You think to yourself, "Are you kidding me, we have great sex, we laugh together and spend all of our waking hours together and now you are telling me you need space. You aren't happy! "What the @#$%^?".

The bottom line is that you had emotional leverage until you liked him more than he liked you. The harder he worked to win you over (**level 2** behavior), the more you let your guard down. You assumed he is really into you because his pursuit seems to lack any hidden agendas. You might have even felt as though you had found your soul mate. The number one reason he disrespects you is that you believe that your **level 2** boyfriend became a **level 1** in your six weeks of dating.

Rule #11 ~ Don't Give Excessive Compliments Unless They Are Going To Improve the Quality of the Relationship

For those in doubt, ask your chocolate, "If I give you excessive compliments and admiration will it lead to excessive dinners, kisses, gifts, or more cuddling?" In most cases he will answer no, not really, or maybe. I'm certain you won't get an absolute yes. Make him earn the compliments he receives. If he is really cool and takes care of you, by all means give him compliments, but don't let the spiritual you lose control over the physical you.

Attractive men hear flattering and flirtatious remarks all day long. Giving out compliments for the sake of it isn't as effective as an intimate compliment. The best time to give him a compliment is when you both are lying down having foreplay or a quite intimate moment. At these times, you have his undivided attention. After sex, he is on to his next goal, sleeping, more sex, watching the game, work, etc. The very worst time to give a compliment is when he is, expecting it or when he gives you a compliment. The reason its bad timing is because he is looking for attention or feels insecure and wants reassurance. The time we all need reassurance is when we are not on top of things and we know in our hearts we half-committed to the task at hand. Instead of feeding into his insecurity, address the real issue that merits him to seek your validation. Ask why he is feeling insecure today? This is very empowering. If he asks how the sex is, say "It is okay, not bad." Don't say, "Oh my God, you are incredible" to make him feel good because he's lacking confidence... ding-ding game over. Just say it is ok. If he said, "I love you, I miss you, and you are incredible", fight the urge to reply with all your heart and say, "I love you <u>too</u>, I miss you <u>too</u>, you are <u>also</u> incredible too," ding-ding, game over you lose.

When someone gives a compliment such as I love you, chances are there is more that follows those three words. The moment you say I love you too; you've cut off their need to express any more emotions. Next time when he says, "I love you," wait a beat and see if he has more to say and if not just say, "Thank you." If your chocolate says, "Aren't you going to say you love me too" your reply is "I'll say it when I feel it" or "I'll say it when I feel the need to say it." There is no obligation for you to reply with the same words. If you can control yourself and keep your composure, your guy is going to be crazy about you.

If you meet a guy in a club or on the street, don't immediately tell him how hot he is. Obviously, you find him attractive because you are talking to him. Don't give compliments for the sake of giving compliments, they should be earned.

Rule #12 ~ Don't Give More Than You Are Getting

Don't give more than you are getting. Keep the playing field even. If he says, I don't think this is working out, agree with him. If he wants to hang with his boys, go and hang with your girls. Do not hang out by the phone waiting for his call. If you are with your girlfriend, don't check your cell phone every ten minutes or turn your evening with your friends into a round table to talk about your boyfriend. Avoid situations where you are sitting at home while he is out playing and getting attention from other women. You make sure you are getting your share of attention from men.

If you are the type of girl that stays home and thinks you don't want to play a games think again. It is a game and you better know the rules. If your guy is out clubbing and you're at home, he is doing it because he wants attention or he is looking for something besides you. Maybe he is bored. Regardless, don't twiddle your thumbs waiting. If he hangs out long enough, he'll find it or it will find him. If he wants to go out, make sure you go out too and have some fun. He will be more interested in what you are doing and less interested in his boy's club.

Remember he needs to earn your affection. The thought of you talking to another man will make him step up his game. He likes competition as long as he is winning. No matter who you flirt with, your guy should always be number one. He'll love the challenge. Keep the playing field equal.

Rule #13 ~ Never Ask If He Is Seeing Someone

This is a tricky one. As much as you want to know, you don't need to ask if he is seeing someone else. You will know sooner or later, especially in the beginning of a relationship. Whether or not he is seeing someone else doesn't evaluate your worth. It shouldn't really matter, especially if you are not in a committed relationship. If you hold yourself in the highest of esteem, he'll respond accordingly. You'll get a direct answer to your question – are you the only one in his life? Asking weak questions doesn't make you seem confident. If he is seeing someone, he will immediately compare you to her. If he is giving you the time of day, the relationship with his current girlfriend probably isn't that strong. Don't ask about the other girl. Talk about how you are going to rock his world.

Instead of asking about the girlfriend, pay attention to the conversation. You will discover things about his past or current relationship that will help you without your having to ask directly. In the subtext of his conversation, he will tell you how he wants to be treated. He might say his ex was a jerk. Ask empowering questions that move the conversation to his being closer to you. This book is about managing yourself and your chocolate. When you are with him, work towards closing the deal. Make yourself available and figure out what his needs are so that he is invested in you. I can assure you the other girl that he might be seeing is not.

Rule #14 ~ Only Compliments During Foreplay / After Sex

Only compliment him when you are having foreplay or during a true moment of intimacy. It is truly the only time you have his undivided attention. That is when you want to place that positive emotional trigger. Until you have emotional leverage and you are in control of yourself, you can't go around throwing compliments. I think the best time to express words of affection is when you have his undivided attention, which is usually during foreplay and after sex.

Rule #15 ~ Give Him Less Attention to Get More

The less attention you give chocolate, the more attention you'll get in return. When you shower him with gifts and attention, he'll show you less respect. It's a strange, but true phenomenon. His disrespect towards you is actually himself saying that he doesn't think he deserves all the attention you are giving. He'll feel better earning your affection instead of it being handed to him on a silver platter. When he earns it he'll be very sweet and attentive, doing all the nice things that you love. You have to learn balance and know when to shower him with affection and when to pull back. If you pay him attention and you see his mood swing away from you, pull back your attention. You'll see his eagerness to please you and you'll see the relationship rebalance itself.

Rule #16 ~ All Booty Calls Requires Condoms

You don't want to catch anything. You don't want to have to explain to your friends and family "It just happened." Need I say more? Until you are in a committed relationship, use a condom even if you are on birth control. No accidents - no babies. No trapping a man into fatherhood for your own needs. Those being: I want to have a baby before it's too late or I want to hold and have him in my life forever, via a child.

Rule #17 ~ Get a Prenuptial Agreement

Get a prenuptial agreement, even if your prenuptial states that everything is 50/50. For the simple reason, you really don't know your partner nor does he really know you. You have no idea what will happen down the road between you and your partner. What if you meet the other guy of your dreams? What if after ten years you really don't like each other? Avoid the drama of divorce, which involves lawyers and court costs. In all aspects of your life you sign contracts and they all explain the consequences if things don't work out. A prenuptial agreement serves the same purpose as any contract.

Epilogue ~

In the end do Mimi and Jake make it as a happy couple? Does Jake go back to his old ways? Does Mimi continue to chase Jake with the hope that she can change him? Will Mimi wait too long until she is too old to have a baby? My guess is that not much will change – Jake and Mimi will continue their on again / off again behavior as long as Mimi will put up with it or until one of them has had enough. Whatever their outcome, don't let your relationship run amuck like theirs.

I hope this book has taught you something about you and your chocolate. If not this book, then maybe another, but learn as much as you can about one of the most important aspects in your life – your relationships. Take your relationships seriously. Time flies and goes from twenty to forty in a wink of an eye. Don't let the myths and hype about relationships get in the way of your happiness and desires. Be okay with your choices – it's your life and you are an adult. Make adult decisions. If you like chocolate, you're not alone.

I wrote this book to inspire current and future generations of women. It's written for you as well as for your daughters, with the hope that they will learn from our mistakes. Let's start a new generation of women who know how to manage themselves in the relationship of their choice and not have to surrender to the default / understudy, but get exactly what they want. I want this book to help women enjoy the type of men they are most attracted to and for them to be happy and not victims of circumstance, like Mimi.

When it comes to matters of the heart, I'd rather not pretend. The more honest you are about your relationship, the situation, and/or circumstance, the better. It gives you truth about yourself and your mate – not your romantic belief that could end in disaster.

As much as we pretend we are not attracted to a certain type, the truth remains we like what we like. Most of us pretend we are not attracted to a certain type as our own way of protecting ourselves from being judged. Who wants negative criticism, especially from the ones we love? It is easier for all of us to pretend and deny our desire if it means escaping judgment. Inside, you want more wild sex from your boyfriend / husband, but you dare not to mention your fantasy because you fear he won't accept you. You don't bring your boyfriend home to meet your parents out of fear he won't live up to their expectations. Pretending and denying our needs won't stop one fundamental fact and that is we like what we like. *IF YOU LIKE CHOCOLATE, EAT CHOCOLATE.*

≈

1603283